THE
EVERYTHING®
Dog Owner's
Organizer

Calendars, checklists, and schedules to
keep your dog happy and healthy

Kim Campbell Thornton and Debra Eldredge, D.V.M.

Adams Media
Avon, Massachusetts

Publishing Director: Gary M. Krebs
Associate Managing Editor: Laura M. Daly
Associate Copy Chief: Brett Palana-Shanahan
Acquisitions Editor: Kate Burgo
Development Editor: Katie McDonough
Associate Production Editor: Casey Ebert

Director of Manufacturing: Susan Beale
Associate Director of Production: Michelle Roy Kelly
Cover Design: Paul Beatrice, Erick DaCosta, Matt LeBlanc
Layout and Graphics: Heather Barrett, Brewster Brownville, Colleen Cunningham, Jennifer Oliveira

🐾 🐾 🐾

Published by Adams Media, an F+W Publications Company
57 Littlefield Street
Avon, MA 02322
www.adamsmedia.com

ISBN 10: 1-59869-099-X
ISBN 13: 978-1-59869-099-6
Printed in China.

J I H G F E D C B A

This book is available at quantity discounts for bulk purchases.
For information, please call 1-800-872-5627.

Contents

Introduction ❧ vii

part one
Welcoming Your Dog . . . 1

chapter 1: Preparing for Your Pup . . . 3

Adjusting Your Lifestyle ❧ 3
Essential Supplies ❧ 5
Puppy-Proofing Your Home ❧ 10
Choosing a Name ❧ 12

chapter 2: Rules and Routines . . . 15

Starting Early ❧ 15
A Family Affair ❧ 16
Create Calendars ❧ 18

chapter 3: Housetraining and Crate Training . . . 23

Housetraining Basics ❧ 23
Crate Training ❧ 24
Create a Schedule ❧ 30
Dealing with Accidents ❧ 33
Charting Progress ❧ 34

part two
Routine Care and Health . . . 39

chapter 4: Bathing and Grooming . . . 41

The Art of the Bath ❧ 41
Brushing Basics and Tools ❧ 43
How to Brush ❧ 46
Nail Trimming ❧ 53
Cleaning Eyes and Ears ❧ 53
Notes and Observations ❧ 54

chapter 5: Nutrition . . . 57

Food Basics ❧ 57
Puppy Nutrition ❧ 64
Adult Dog Nutrition ❧ 66
A Feeding Schedule ❧ 70

chapter 6: Veterinary Care . . . 75

The Veterinary Visit ❧ 75
Vaccinations ❧ 78
Medications ❧ 88
Spay/Neuter Surgery ❧ 92

chapter 7: Your Dog's Health . . . 99

Signs of Illness ❧ 99
Recognizing Pain ❧ 105
Managing Pain ❧ 110
External Parasites ❧ 114
Internal Parasites ❧ 127

part three
Exercise, Socialization, and Training . . . 139

chapter 8: Exercise and Play . . . 141

Exercise Guidelines ❀ 141
Create a Schedule ❀ 142
Sports and Exercise Programs ❀ 144
Warm Up and Cool Down ❀ 150
Dealing with Injuries ❀ 151
Notes and Observations ❀ 156

chapter 9: Socializing Your Dog . . . 159

Exploring the Environment ❀ 159
Meeting People ❀ 162
Meeting Other Animals ❀ 164
Riding in the Car ❀ 166
Socializing Safely ❀ 167
Dealing with a Fearful Dog ❀ 167

chapter 10: Basic and Obedience Training . . . 175

Training Basics ❀ 175
Getting Started ❀ 181
Obedience Training ❀ 183
The Learning Process ❀ 200

part four
Uniquely Yours . . . 207

   chapter 11: About Your Dog . . . 209

   Keep a Record ❧ 209
   Photos ❧ 220

   chapter 12: Contact Information . . . 243

   appendix A: Journal Pages . . . 249
   appendix B: Resources . . . 257
   appendix C: Frequently Asked Questions
              and Vet Answers . . . 265

Introduction

Dog ownership is one of the greatest experiences a person can have. Dogs give the kind of unconditional love and companionship that few pets—and people!—can offer. The downside, however, is that caring for a dog is a big responsibility. Sometimes it feels like your dog is your child—you always want to do what's best for him. But the reality is that people who work and/or raise a family rarely have lots of free time and energy. Perhaps you're used to haphazardly storing your dog's paperwork in random folders and drawers. You have trouble remembering how long you exercised Spike yesterday, and you have no idea when his last veterinary check up was. This organizer is the answer to your problems! Its purpose is to help you be a more relaxed, confident dog owner, so you can spend your free time playing Frisbee with Spike instead of hunting for his missing vaccination records.

Whether you've just gotten a ten-week-old puppy or you're looking to become a better owner for your seven-year-old adult dog, this organizer can help you achieve your goals. Chapters 1, 2, and 3 will tell you all you need to know to prepare for your new pup and will give you a chance to keep track of everything from his reactions to grooming to his housetraining progress. Chapters 4 and 5 will help you organize a bathing and grooming routine and create a feeding schedule for your dog. You can write right in this organizer in the spaces provided and use the note-taking sections to jot down anything of interest. Keep the organizer in a safe, accessible place, and refer to it anytime you need to check medical records, look up the groomer's phone number, or see whose day it is to feed the dog.

One of your most important tasks as a dog owner is to keep your pet healthy. Working with your veterinarian can help you ensure that your dog lives a long, happy life, and you can work together toward preventing health problems before they begin. Knowing your dog's habits is a good place to start. When you know his normal eating, sleeping, and exercise routines, recognizing a problem is easier. Any change in your dog's normal routine may indicate a problem and should sound an alarm for you to keep a close eye on him. Luckily, this organizer provides a place for you to document your dog's normal state, as well as any changes in him. Chapter 6 will help you keep track of your dog's vaccinations and medications, as well as the details surrounding spay or neuter surgery. Chapter 7 focuses on your dog's general health, offering you the chance to record illnesses and injures, as well as encounters with parasites like fleas and ticks. Once all of the information is filled in, this organizer will make a great reference tool for veterinary appointments.

Making sure your dog is healthy and happy also means exercising and socializing him. Chapters 8 and 9 offer lots of great tools on these topics—from exercise schedules to socialization plans—that will help you create a consistent, enjoyable routine for your dog. You can even make copies of your schedules, calendars, and checklists and post them on the refrigerator or a bulletin board as a reference for everyone in the household. This is one of many fun ways to get the whole family involved with your pet's care.

The goal of this organizer is to help you take the best possible care of your dog so that the two of you will share a long, lasting, and loving relationship. So, turn the page and start becoming a more organized dog owner today. Your pup will thank you!

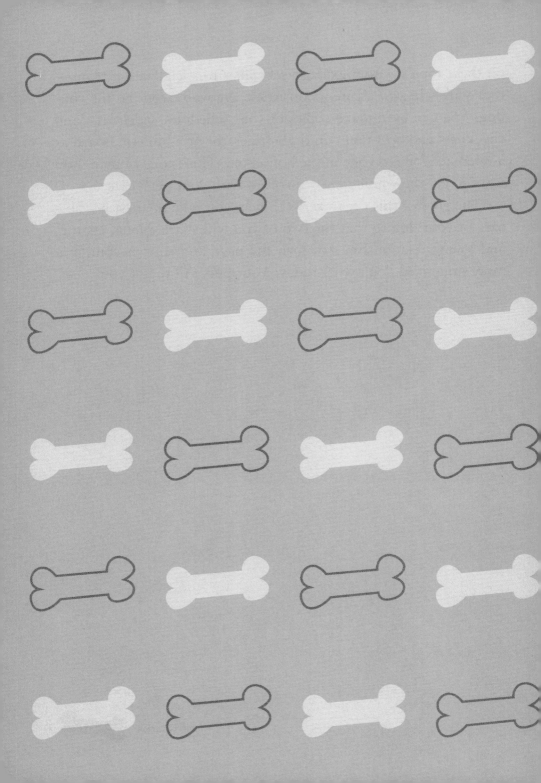

part one

Welcoming Your Dog

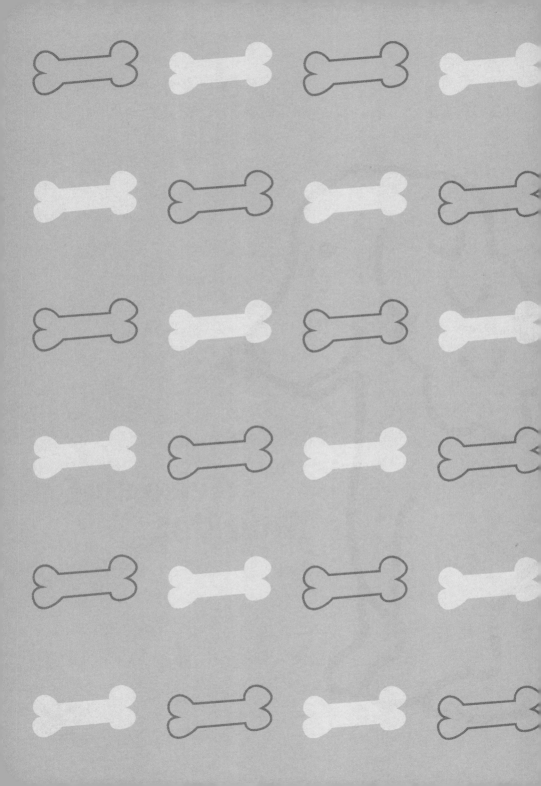

chapter 1

Preparing for Your Pup

Adjusting Your Lifestyle

Introducing a dog into your family's life is a joyful and exciting experience, but it is not something to be done on a whim. You must mentally, financially, and otherwise prepare yourself for the numerous responsibilities that come with caring for a dog. Furthermore, everyone in your household needs to be in agreement with the decision.

Before deciding to get a dog, and even before deciding what breed of dog to get, consider your current lifestyle, home, and habits. Answer the following questions to see how well you would adjust to dog ownership:

Are you a good housekeeper who would not mind adding vacuuming up dog hair and mopping up muddy paw prints to your list of weekly chores?

Is anyone in your family allergic to dogs? If so, are you willing to pursue the necessary adjustments, such as allergy medications and air purifiers?

_____

Does your current budget allow for a dog's ongoing necessities, such as food, veterinary checkups, and medications? If not, what budget adjustments do you plan to make?

_____

Do you have enough yard space (or a nearby park) where the dog can get daily exercise?

_____

Will each member of the family share the responsibility of your dog's care equally, or will one or two people be in charge of all his needs?

_____

If your answers to these questions indicate that you're prepared for dog ownership, the next step is to determine what general size and breed of dog you're interested in and able to accommodate. Weigh all factors of a breed carefully, including those that follow. Write down what you know about the breed you're considering for each point, and star those that are still in question.

- Size _____

- Grooming requirements _____

- Exercise needs _____

- Special equipment needs (such as a very large crate for a giant-breed dog) _____

- Ease of training _____

- Behavior around children _____

- Temperament (friend to all or a bit of a guard dog?) _____

- Activities you may want to share with your dog, such as agility or obedience _____

Luckily, dogs have an incredibly wide range of variation. There are purebred dogs of virtually every possible size, coat, color, and temperament combination. When you add in the amazing mixed breeds, there is sure to be a pup somewhere that is just right for you!

Essential Supplies

Your new pup will need a set of basic supplies to help her settle into your home. First of all, a crate is very important. This is a metal or plastic cage that serves as your pup's bedroom. She will sleep in this at first, take naps here, and rest safely while you are busy or away from home. A crate can double as a safe carrier on car trips or airline flights. It will also help with housetraining—puppies don't like to mess in *their* room, even if they don't mind going on your best rug! For this reason, make sure the crate is big enough for your pup to lie comfortably and turn around in, but not so big that she can divide it into an area for messing and an area for sleeping.

A crate can be moved around your house so your pup can still be involved with the family, even at night or during mealtimes, and it also serves to keep your pup safe. If you are busy and can't be watching her closely, your pup could be chewing on poisonous plants, biting into electrical cords, or eating dangerous household items. Tucked into her crate with a blanket and a chew toy, she is safe—and so is your house! It is very sad to learn of puppies left tied out behind the house alone because they did damage in the house. That is a much crueler fate than resting in a crate for a few hours. For them it is a safe den—a quiet retreat from guests, too much activity, and other pets.

As you might guess, there are different types of crates on the market, as well as various options when it comes to other dog essentials. Refer to the following chart as you begin to collect the main items your new dog needs.

Item	Material	What's Best?
Crate	Plastic or wire	A plastic crate offers privacy and is good for air travel. A wire crate provides good ventilation and can be folded for storage, but it's not suited for air travel.
Collar	Leather, canvas, nylon, or chain	Choose a collar with a buckle, plastic snap, or safety release—not a chain or prong collar. Slip chains, prong collars, and head halters may all be useful for a teenage "juvenile delinquent" dog but are not appropriate for a young puppy. They should only be used under the guidance of your veterinarian or an experienced trainer.
Leash	Leather, canvas, nylon, or chain	Leather and canvas are easiest on the hands. Flexible and retractable leashes are not good for use with puppies. These retractable leads can be good for exercising a dog that has been trained not to pull. Do not let a dog on one of these leads get around a corner or where you can't see him.
Bed	Anything from a cedar-filled pillow to an old comforter	Go with what your pup prefers, as long as it's washable.
Food and water bowls	Stainless steel, plastic, glass, or ceramic	Stainless steel is nonallergenic (unlike some plastics), durable, and easy to clean. Avoid anything that could break under the foot of a clumsy puppy.

Item	Details
Brush	A thin hound-cloth works for dogs with short, tight coats, such as greyhounds, while a long-coated dog like a collie may need a slicker brush and a pin brush. Talk to your breeder or the shelter staff about the right brushes for your pup.
Nail clippers	To clip a dog's nails, you need special dog nail clippers. Styptic powder is also a good idea in case of bleeding.
Toothbrush	You can buy toothbrushes for dogs, but a child's soft toothbrush will work just as well.
Toothpaste	Human toothpaste does not appeal to dogs and is not meant to be swallowed. Instead, get some special dog toothpaste in a choice flavor, such as poultry.
Cotton balls	Cotton balls can be used for routinely cleaning your dog's ears. Lightly moisten the cotton before gently wiping the outer ear.
Towels	It's good to have some extra "dog towels" to dry her off after a walk in the rain or an encounter with the sprinkler.

Once you have a collar, you need to add identification tags to help your pup return home if she gets lost, and a rabies tag, once she is vaccinated. Microchips, which are inserted under the skin with a needle, are another identification option. Each tiny chip has a unique number that can be read with a scanner. This number is linked to the information necessary to return your dog home. With a collar with tags and a microchip, your dog is doubly protected if she gets lost. Tags are visible, but they can fall off or be removed. A microchip provides backup identification if this happens.

Grooming Tools

Grooming equipment varies among different breeds, but every dog needs to have her coat brushed, nails clipped, teeth brushed, and ears cleaned. The following list on the next page contains useful grooming tools you need for your dog

Toys

Favorite toys will vary from dog to dog. A tiny Chihuahua pup may not be interested in a tennis ball, while a Labrador retriever will be thrilled. Make sure the toys are "puppy safe," that is, filled with nontoxic stuffing. Plastic that will break is not safe. Make sure your pup doesn't swallow any squeakers if she is tearing up a toy. With the exception of toys like Kongs and Gumabones or Nylabones, which are exceptionally tough, very few toys should be left with an unsupervised pup.

Puppy-Proofing Your Home

Keeping your puppy and your home safe from each other can be a challenge. Your goal is to keep your pup with you as much as possible. Supervision is the key to prevention, as is keeping your pup out of places where he can cause trouble.

In general, be sure that all valuable items are kept out of the dog's reach. Shoes need to be in closets with closed doors. Books need to be kept safe high up on shelves or in storage boxes. Also remember that breakable items will not only break if they fall from tables or countertops, but they will also shatter into a thousand pieces. These pieces could scratch up your floors or get stuck in carpeting, only to prick someone's bare feet—or paws—later.

It's important that you involve your children in the puppy-proofing plans as well. Kids are notorious for leaving their belongings around the house, and a young pup will only see their dolls and games as great chew toys. Now is a great time to set up a system for keeping toys and games stowed away in the proper places. Toy chests with heavy lids work well, and storage crates that can be stowed in closets are also good options. Here are some other great items to have on hand for storing things out of paws' reach:

- ❧ **SHOEBOXES:** The lids keep contents from pouring out, and the boxes stack neatly on shelves. Label the side of the box so you can tell what's inside even when it's stored in the closet.

- ❧ **PLASTIC MILK CRATES:** Because they're so rugged, these crates are great for storing sporting equipment like Frisbees, soccer cleats, and baseball gloves in closets.

❧   **JARS (FROM SALSA, PEANUT BUTTER, ETC.):** A clean jar with a lid is great tool for storing the small pieces that come with some kids' toys. The clear glass or plastic allows you to see what's inside, and the lid will keep the small items from spilling onto the floor where a curious puppy can scarf them up.

Review the following checklist as you begin puppy-proofing your home:

☐   **INVEST IN BABY GATES.** These adjustable gates can block off doorways, separate combative pets, or keep your pup off your heirloom Oriental rug.

☐   **STOW DANGEROUS HOUSEHOLD ITEMS.** Cleaning products and other toxic substances, such as bleach, should be in locked cupboards.

☐   **COVER OR HIDE ELECTRICAL CORDS.** All cords need to be moved out of reach or covered with thick plastic hosing for extra protection.

☐   **CLEAR COUNTERS AND TABLETOPS.** A large-breed pup will quickly grow big enough to reach these areas, so clear them of all items you don't want him to have.

☐   **PROTECT FURNITURE LEGS.** If your pup has a penchant for furniture legs, coat them with Bitter Apple. The paste form often works better than the spray.

Choosing a Name

A cozy crate, fluffy bed, and colorful collar will make your new pet feel right at home, but he still needs a name! As a part of your family, your dog must have an identity, and for practical purposes, you need a way to call him.

Perhaps you chose the perfect name well in advance of your pup's arrival. Or maybe you want to wait to meet your pup before deciding on a name. Either way, it's good to have some idea of what you'd like to call your dog before you bring him home. The following list from *www.petrix.com/dognames* contains the top ten most popular dog names in North America:

1. Sam, Sammie, or Samantha
2. Max, Maxie, Maxwell, or Maxine
3. Lady
4. Bear
5. Maggie
6. Buddy
7. Tasha
8. Chelsea or Chelsie
9. Holly
10. Shasta

This Web site also contains an alphabetized list of 2,000 dog names for you to consider as you prepare for your new pet. Use the following spaces to keep track of the names you're considering:

MALE NAMES

_____

_____

_____

_____

_____

_____

_____

_____

_____

_____

FEMALE NAMES

_____

_____

_____

_____

_____

_____

_____

_____

_____

_____

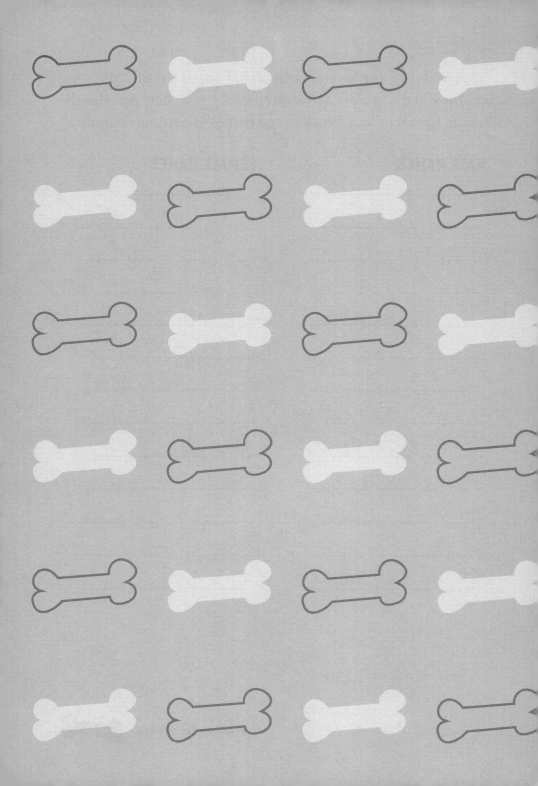

chapter 2

Rules and Routines

Starting Early

Just like human babies, puppies do best when given rules and a routine to follow. (While we say puppy here, a new adult dog such as an adult from a shelter or rescue group will need to follow the same routines as a puppy at first.) This keeps the fussing to a minimum and really helps with housetraining. Keep in mind that your pup has no sense of the days of the week. If you get up at 6 A.M. on Monday through Friday to give her a short walk and breakfast, you can't expect her to sleep in until 8 A.M. on Saturday. Think of it this way—you have even more hours to enjoy your new companion!

The following list contains some great ways to start setting rules and creating routines for your pup from the very beginning. Everyone must agree on these things so the pup doesn't get confused.

☐ **KEEP HER ON LEASH, EVEN INDOORS.** This will keep your pup from wandering and getting into trouble, but it will still allow more freedom than her crate. It will also teach her to learn to look to you for guidance.

☐ **CHOOSE A FEEDING TIME AND STICK TO IT.** It's important that the dog is fed twice daily at around the same time. This will help her learn to trust and rely on you.

☐ **SET FURNITURE BOUNDARIES.** Decide whether or not the pup is allowed on the furniture. If so, is she only allowed on certain furniture, while other pieces are off limits?

☐ **CREATE SLEEPING RULES.** Decide whether the pup will sleep on the bed of a family member or on her own bed on the floor.

It might seem cute now for your little Saint Bernard pup to curl up on your lap to watch television, but that might not be so fun when your pup is a 150-pound adult. Decide on house rules now, and make sure the whole family sticks to them!

A Family Affair

Dog ownership involves everyone in your household, including even the youngest child. Therefore, everyone needs to be taught how to handle the new dog, possibly even before his arrival. If you have children, try out the following activities to teach them the responsibility of caring for a dog.

Activity	What to Do
Practice pup	Have each child care for a stuffed toy for a week. This can include always knowing where the toy is, having "feeding time" every day, and setting aside some time for petting and attention.
Baggie and biscuit	Teach children that when the dog goes to the bathroom in a public outdoor area, the mess needs to be picked up. Show them how to pick up poop in a baggie, seal it, and dispose of it. During housetraining time, remind them to give the dog a treat when she goes to the bathroom outside.
Pick up the pup	Children rarely know the correct way to hold a puppy, so be sure you teach them. Have them reach under the pup's chest between his front legs with one hand and place the fingers of the other hand between his two rear legs, keeping the thumb under his tail. Have them hold him close to their chest so he can lean into them.
Basic training	As you teach your dog his basic skills, like sit and stay, be sure your children also know how to give these commands. Kids will enjoy being involved and showing off their dog's skills to friends.

Create Calendars

Organization is key when you have a playful new pup to care for. Calendars are a great way to start creating schedules and assigning duties. Use the following four calendar templates to delegate exercise, feeding, bathing and grooming, and training responsibilities among your family members.

First is the exercise calendar. Perhaps you would like to walk the dog on Tuesdays, Thursdays, and Sundays while your children will split up the remaining days of the week. Next is the feeding calendar. If your spouse gets home from work earlier than you do, perhaps he or she can feed the dog on weekdays while you cover weekends. The third calendar is the bathing and grooming calendar. Obviously a dog doesn't need to be bathed as often as he needs to be groomed, but it's still important to keep a schedule for both duties. Perhaps you will bathe the dog every other Saturday and your children will take turns brushing him every other day after school. Finally, the training calendar can be used to mark who will work on training the dog on what day. To be successful with dog training, you must be consistent. Perhaps you and your son will work on training on Tuesdays, Thursdays, and Saturdays, and your spouse and daughter will take care of the remaining days of the week.

Make copies of the calendars and post them on the refrigerator, a bulletin board, or in a similarly visible location. This will help you get off to a solid start with your new dog. You'll find other calendars and schedules later in the book to help you stay organized as you progress with activities like exercise and training.

Exercise Calendar

SUNDAY	MONDAY	TUESDAY	WEDNES-DAY	THURSDAY	FRIDAY	SATURDAY

Feeding Calendar

SUNDAY	MONDAY	TUESDAY	WEDNES-DAY	THURSDAY	FRIDAY	SATURDAY

The Everything Dog Owner's Organizer

Bathing and Grooming Calendar

SUNDAY	MONDAY	TUESDAY	WEDNES-DAY	THURSDAY	FRIDAY	SATURDAY

Training Calendar

SUNDAY	MONDAY	TUESDAY	WEDNES-DAY	THURSDAY	FRIDAY	SATURDAY

The Everything Dog Owner's Organizer

chapter 3

Housetraining and Crate Training

Housetraining Basics

The first thing every new owner should know before bringing a puppy or adult dog (such as a shelter or rescue dog) into the house is how to teach her where to relieve herself. The good news is that all puppies can be housetrained. The bad news is that a puppy rarely becomes housetrained by just being let out several times a day. This comprehensive housetraining plan requires dedication—but it's simple and foolproof. Here are the basics:

* Confine your puppy to her crate when you can't watch her so she won't relieve herself where she's not supposed to or while you're not looking. (If you prefer, use a baby gate to confine her to the kitchen or laundry room while you can't watch her–just make sure the room is puppy-proofed.)

* Supervise your puppy when she is out of her crate.

- Feed her a high-quality diet at scheduled times and limit treats.

- Take her to her potty spot as soon as you return home, soon after meals, and when she wakes up from a nap.

- Teach her to eliminate on command by saying "Go potty, good puppy" in an excited voice while she's doing her business.

- Clean up her accidents immediately (remove debris or moisture, then treat with neutralizer and cleaner).

- Never correct her after the fact.

- Keep a log of her habits (when and where she pooped or peed, and when and how much she ate and drank).

Crate Training

Until a puppy is perfectly trained, she needs a safe place in which she can do nothing wrong. So when you can't keep your eyes glued to your puppy and monitor her every move, confine her to a place where inappropriate behavior—soiling, stealing, shredding, chewing, or scratching—isn't an option. Crating is best because it eliminates the risk of her damaging woodwork, flooring, wall covering, or cabinetry.

Assuming you ultimately want your puppy to enjoy freedom in the house, crating is almost a rearing necessity. Crating is widely accepted by behaviorists, puppy trainers, veterinarians, and knowledgeable puppy owners as a humane means of confinement. Provided your puppy is properly introduced to her crate, you should feel as comfortable about crating her in your absence as you would securing a toddler in a highchair at mealtime.

Whether the enclosure is a room, hallway, kennel, or crate, it should be all of the following:

- **THE RIGHT SIZE:** It should be large enough that when your puppy is a full-grown dog she'll be able to stand without her shoulders touching the ceiling of the crate. This size crate will be far too large for your puppy at first. Use a divider to limit the amount of space your puppy has; for the first month or so, one-third to one-half the crate should be fine.

- **SAFE:** Homemade enclosures may save you money, but you would feel awful if she poked herself in the eye, stabbed or hung herself, or swallowed wood splinters or material like wallpaper or blankets because you ignored potential dangers. Make sure there are no protrusions or sharp edges, and no ingestible components.

- **PUPPY-PROOF:** If she is prone to chewing, scratching or jumping up, prevent access to any woodwork, linoleum, furniture, counters, garbage, or windows so your home doesn't become a victim of your puppy's destructiveness during her training period.

Introducing Puppy to the Crate

Though your puppy will come to think of her crate as her sanctuary because it satisfies her natural denning instinct, she may not like the idea of going in the crate at first. If you reinforce her objections to the crate by making her early associations with it unpleasant, she may never adjust to it. And that will be a setback for both of you. Go slowly, and praise every positive step along the way. Check off the following points as you complete them, and take notes on any specific behaviors you notice.

☐ PUT THE CRATE SOMEWHERE YOUR PUP WILL HAVE SOME PRIVACY, BUT NOT WHERE SHE'LL FEEL ALONE. A CORNER OF THE KITCHEN IS USUALLY A GOOD SPOT.

_____

_____

☐ LINE THE BOTTOM OF THE CRATE WITH NEWSPAPER FOR EXTRA INSULATION FROM THE COLD FLOOR. THEN PUT A SOFT BLANKET OR PIECE OF FLEECE ON TOP OF THE NEWSPAPER. THE BLANKET OR FLEECE SHOULD BE MACHINE WASHABLE, AS ACCIDENTS WILL PROBABLY HAPPEN IN THE BEGINNING.

_____

_____

☐ GET YOUR PUPPY INTO A GOOD CHEW-TOY HABIT RIGHT AWAY BY PUTTING AN APPROPRIATE CHEW TOY IN THE CRATE. PUPPIES NEED TO CHEW, SO UNLESS YOU WANT THEM TO GO TO WORK ON YOUR SHOES, FURNITURE, OR FLOOR, TURN THEM ON TO PUPPY-APPROPRIATE TOYS EARLY.

_____

_____

☐ WHEN HER CRATE IS PREPARED, CALL HER OVER TO IT. DON'T PUSH HER TOWARD IT OR INTO IT. MAKE IT INTERESTING BY PUTTING SOME SMALL BITS OF SOMETHING TASTY LIKE COLD CUTS NEAR THE ENTRANCE. WHEN SHE SHOWS INTEREST, TOSS A GOODY INTO THE CRATE. IF SHE RUNS IN AND GOBBLES IT UP, TELL HER WHAT A GOOD PUPPY SHE IS.

_____

_____

☐ DON'T SHUT THE DOOR ON HER THE FIRST TIME SHE GOES IN THE CRATE. LET HER GO IN AND OUT A FEW TIMES, CONTINUING TO PRAISE WHEN SHE SHOWS INTEREST. AFTER ALL THIS STIMULATION, TAKE HER TO HER POTTY SPOT. THIS IS HER FIRST INTRODUCTION TO THE CRATE.

_____

_____

Later, feed your puppy in the crate. Place her and her food inside and sit with your back blocking the doorway of the crate. Don't close the crate door. For her next meal, prop the crate door and sit at the opening with your puppy. Keeping her food in the bowl, place a few pieces of kibble in the crate, then feed her a few pieces from your hand outside the crate. This way she associates being fed as something that happens in the crate and out. Feeding your puppy from your hands is also an excellent way to teach her that your hands mean good things. Your puppy (and later, your dog) should always associate your hands (and any person's hands) coming toward her as a good thing. There may be times when you have to grab her collar or take her food away or when strangers want to pet her.

Going to Bed

Next, teach your puppy to enter and exit the crate on command using the following steps:

1. Put her paws right in front of the opening.
2. With one hand on her collar and the other pointing into the crate, say, "Bed."
3. Gently guide her in by the collar as you place your hand under her tail and behind her rear legs to prevent her from backing away. If necessary, gently lift her in. When she's in, say "Good bed!" and give her a treat.
4. Immediately invite her out by saying, "Okay," and praising her for coming out to you.

Practice several repetitions of this routine—without shutting your pup in the crate. If you shut her in and leave her every time she is put in the enclosure, she may develop a bad association with crating. But when she learns to go in the crate on command as a result of frequent practice, she is more likely to also accept being enclosed. Make sure to give her some treats while she is in the crate as well.

Crate Soiling

Although dogs normally won't mess in their crates, some do. Occasional accidents shouldn't concern you, but if it happens every other day or more, try these suggestions:

* Remove all bedding. Believe it or not, it may repulse her to have nothing to absorb the mess and motivate her to hold it until you let her out.

* Use a smaller crate so she only has enough room to turn in place.

* Teach her to enter and exit her crate on command. ("Go to your bed/spot.")

* Put her food and water in the open crate to encourage a better association about being in there; remove it when she's enclosed.

Create a Schedule

Most puppies leave their litter to enter their new home at about two months of age. At this age, the pups eat a lot, drink a lot, and have limited ability to control their elimination and no comprehension that that might be important. Feeding and potty times should be adjusted to help puppy reach her potential in the housetraining department as quickly as possible. At two to four months of age most pups need to relieve themselves after waking up, eating, playing, sleeping, and drinking. At four months, the puppy may be developed like an adult internally, but you should expect her to behave like a puppy.

To housetrain effectively, you need to establish a schedule that works for your family and will help your puppy learn the rules quickly. You will be amazed at how quickly your puppy learns if you stick to a schedule that has fixed times for eating, sleeping, and exercising. Here's a sample schedule:

Time	What to Do
6:30 A.M.	Take puppy out immediately when you wake up
6:45 A.M.	Feed puppy breakfast
7:00 A.M.	Take puppy back outside
7:15 A.M.	Play with puppy while getting ready for the day
7:45 A.M.	Take puppy outside
8:00 A.M.	Crate puppy when family leaves
Noon	Take puppy outside
12:15 P.M.	Feed puppy lunch
12:30 P.M.	Take puppy outside
12:45 P.M.	Play with puppy
1:00 P.M.	Crate puppy if leaving home again; keep her on leash if doing things around the house
5:00 P.M.	Take puppy outside
5:30 P.M.	Feed puppy dinner
5:45 P.M.	Take puppy outside
6:00 P.M.	Play with puppy for remainder of evening, with trips outside every few hours
Just before bedtime	Take puppy outside. No more water after this for the rest of the night. Crate puppy for the night. (Very young puppies may have to be taken out once during the night.)

Using the previous sample as a model, create a housetraining schedule that works for you in the following template. Once you've finalized the schedule, make a copy and post it in a visible area, such as on the refrigerator. This way, everyone can refer to it during those first weeks of housetraining time.

Time	What to Do

Dealing with Accidents

No matter how careful you are, housetraining accidents will occasionally happen. If your pup does have an accident, do not correct him after the fact. Simply examine why the accident might have happened and correct possible mistakes for next time. Clean up the mess immediately. Remove debris and blot up any moisture. Use a cleaning solution, and finally treat the soiled area with an odor neutralizer.

Until your puppy is perfectly potty-trained, remember these things:

* Puppies who can hold it for long periods while they're in their crate or at night are not necessarily well on their way to being housebroken. Don't judge his capacity by his behavior while crated. As a rule, the maximum time a dog should be left in a crate without a break is four to six hours.

* Puppies enjoy playing, observing, and investigating, and they often forget about going potty when they're left alone outdoors. Don't let your puppy out without supervision and assume that he did his business. Take him out on leash so you can make sure he eliminates–praise him when he does so.

* Puppies often indicate when they want to go outdoors and play instead of when they need to potty. Don't rely on or encourage him to tell you he wants to go out. Many puppies that show the desire to go out frequently will always eliminate when taken to the potty area. This causes bladder and bowel capacity and control to be underdeveloped.

Charting Progress

Plan on a year or more to complete the housetraining process. Although your puppy may be flawless for days, weeks, or months, any puppy can backslide under certain conditions. Seemingly benign events such as the following can cause housetraining regression:

- 🐾 Changes in diet can upset the digestive system.

- 🐾 Weather changes (too hot, cold, or wet, or noisy–such as thunderstorms) can make potty outings unproductive.

- 🐾 New environments (vacation homes, new house, or friend's house) may be treated as an extension of his potty area.

- 🐾 Some medications (like allergy medications) and certain conditions (like hormone changes associated with estrus) can cause more frequent elimination.

To keep track of your pup's housetraining progress, fill out the following chart during the first twelve weeks of housetraining. For each week, mark down the dates, the number of accidents (if any), and any notes about your dog's progress. These notes might include how your dog is reacting to the training, the areas where he has made the most improvement, or advice for the next family member scheduled to work on training. Make a copy of the chart and post it somewhere visible where the whole family can contribute and refer to it.

Week of Housetraining	Dates	Number of Accidents	Notes
Week 1			
Week 2			
Week 3			
Week 4			
Week 5			
Week 6			

Week of Housetraining	Dates	Number of Accidents	Notes
Week 7			
Week 8			
Week 9			
Week 10			
Week 11			
Week 12			

Week of Housetraining	Dates	Number of Accidents	Notes
Week 13			
Week 14			
Week 15			
Week 16			
Week 17			
Week 18			

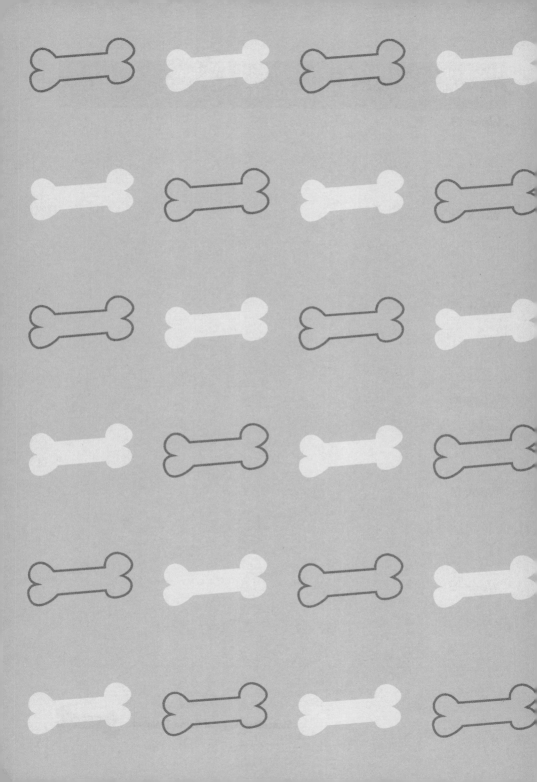

PART 2

Routine Care and Health

Bathing and Grooming

Nutrition

Veterinary Care

Your Dog's Health

part two
Routine
Care and Health

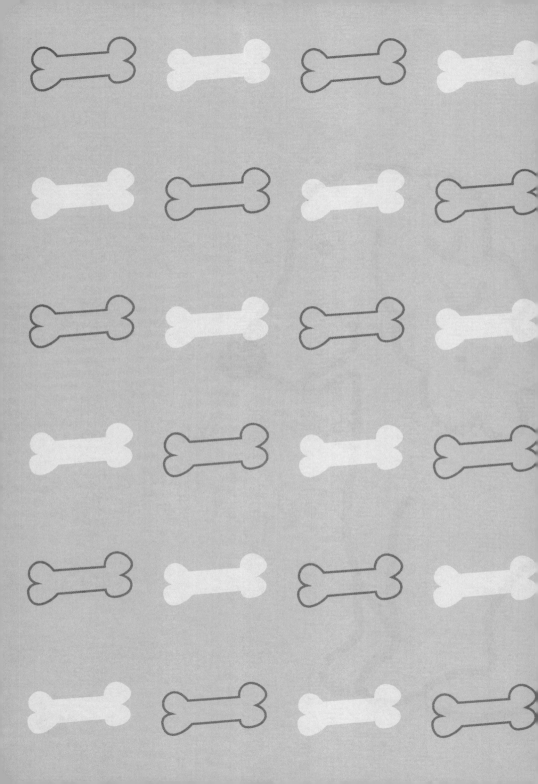

chapter 4

Bathing and Grooming

The Art of the Bath

There are two truths about giving a dog a bath: (1) It's easier if you're organized; and (2) Even if you're organized, you will still get wet. When getting organized, be sure to gather everything you'll need before you even think about running water and calling your dog. That means two to three towels; a washcloth for cleaning the face; cotton balls for inside the ears; mineral oil to put around the eyes to protect them from soapy water; dog shampoo (and conditioner if you use it); a rubber mat to place in the floor of the tub or shower to provide sure footing; and a blow dryer that's plugged in and ready to go wherever you plan to dry the dog.

Step by Step

First things first: Never call your dog to come for a bath (or anything else unpleasant, such as getting medication). She'll quickly get the idea that coming when you call is a bad idea. Instead, go and get her. That way, she won't associate the "Come" command with doing something she doesn't like. Of course, if your dog loves getting baths, this advice doesn't apply.

Follow these procedural steps to ensure bathing success:

1. Begin by brushing your dog thoroughly. Work out any mats or tangles you find. If they get wet, they'll tighten up and become even more difficult to remove.

2. Take your dog to the bath area. A large walk-in shower with a seat and a handheld nozzle is ideal for your small or medium-size dog. Small dogs (up to about twenty pounds) can also be bathed in the kitchen sink, which is easier on your back than bending over a tub.

3. To repel water, dab mineral oil around the eyes, and place cotton balls inside the ears.

4. Wet your dog down to the skin with warm water, starting at the head and working your way back.

5. Apply shampoo, again starting at the head and working back. Massage it in thoroughly. Rinse with warm water until no more suds are running out of the coat. Shampoo that remains in the coat can make it look dull and flaky, so rinse thoroughly. Apply conditioner, if desired, and rinse again.

6. Grab a towel and start drying your dog. Stop for a minute to let her shake out excess water. If you have a longhaired dog, squeeze the water out of the hair on the ears, legs, and tail. By now your first towel is probably pretty wet, so grab another one and dry your dog some more before you let her out of the shower or tub.

Drying Time

Blow-drying your dog is best done with him on a grooming table, picnic table, or other surface that puts him at eye level. It's easier on your back and allows you to dry him more thoroughly. If you have a small dog, an option is to sit on the floor of the bathroom with the dog in your lap and blow-dry him from that position. Whichever spot you choose, be sure your dog can't get away. This means using the noose on the grooming table, closing the door of the bathroom, or having a helper hold the dog while you dry her.

Set the dryer on warm, not hot. Hold it several inches away from your dog's body, and keep it moving so you don't accidentally burn the skin. Brush through the coat as you dry to remove more loose hair, using a curry brush for shorthaired dogs and a pin brush for longhaired dogs. You can dry her completely, or you can get her mostly dry and let her finish drying in her crate. Just be sure the crate is not in the path of any drafts.

When you finally turn her loose, she'll probably go running through the house, rolling on the carpet in an attempt to rid herself of the funny shampoo/conditioner smell. And be warned: If you let her outdoors right after a bath, she'll probably go roll in the first dirty spot she can find.

Brushing Basics and Tools

Regular bathing will do a lot to remove excess hair, rejuvenate skin, and eliminate odors, but frequent brushing is also a must. It promotes blood circulation and new hair growth. A complete canine grooming session involves brushing and combing the coat;

checking the skin for signs of itchiness, parasites, or injuries; cleaning the eyes and ears; and taking care of the nails.

Grooming can be a wonderful time for you to bond with your new pup. By creating a grooming routine, your pup will learn to expect and even enjoy the time with you. Start by just gently using a soft brush or cloth to rub over your pup's back. If she resists, try a few different methods to calm her. Use the following table to keep track of what your dog responds to. Try the various methods and then mark if the response is positive or negative.

Method	Response (Positive or Negative)
Speaking in a positive, high-pitched voice	
Giving treats	
Petting or rubbing on head	
Petting or rubbing on body	
Petting or rubbing on belly	
Brushing lightly	
Brushing with some pressure (massage-like)	

If you have a longhaired pup, try to do just a little grooming every day. That way the pup isn't bored, and you stay on top of any tangles or mats. If you are not willing to take care of a long coat, such as that on a Shih Tzu, you should make the commitment for regular grooming or clipping appointments with a professional groomer.

Your Tool of Choice

Different types of coats require different types of brushes and combs. In fact, your dog might even need a different brush in the summer than in the winter. The following chart will guide you as you make the right brush or comb purchase.

Type of Brush or Comb	Recommended Use
Slicker brush	This brush has fine wire bristles and is especially useful for removing mats and tangles.
Pin brush	This is a wire-pin brush with or without rubber-tipped ends. It's good for dogs with medium to long hair and those with silky, curly, or wooly coats. Flexible pin brushes are also good for pets with thin coats and/or sensitive skin.
Bristle brush	This can be used on all types of coats and is best used for finishing touches after other brushes are used. This is great for small dogs and dogs with sensitive skin.
Curry brush	Also known as a hound mitt or glove, this brush has rubber nubs that massage the skin and loosen excess hair. It will usually have a strap to help you keep a firm grip when brushing. This is good for most shorthaired dogs.
Shedding or dematting comb	This helps break a mat into manageable sections so they can be combed through. Use this before using your brush of choice.

How Often?

Simply to keep shedding at a manageable level, most dogs should be brushed daily. Depending on your dog's coat type, size, and lifestyle, grooming can take as little as five minutes to as much as twenty or more minutes each day. Among the breeds that shed heavily are German shepherds, Dalmatians, Labrador retrievers, and pugs. They have coarse hairs that weave themselves into fabrics and are difficult to remove. By brushing daily, more hair goes onto the brush and into the trash instead of floating off onto furniture and clothing. If your shorthaired dog doesn't shed heavily, a weekly brushing is sufficient.

How to Brush

When you brush, make sure that you are not just brushing the hair on the dog's back. You need to hold the hair up, brush underneath down to the belly, and even brush out any feathering on the legs. Many pups enjoy a good belly rub, and that can be a good time to do a little grooming there, too. The tail needs to be gently brushed, as well as the area around the face and ears. Even short-coated dogs need a wipe with a damp cloth to pick up loose hair and any dirt buildup.

When brushing, don't just lightly run the brush over the top of the coat. Brush all the way down to the skin to remove dirt, skin-cell debris, and loose hairs. You may be amazed at the amount of hair you remove. This is a good grooming task for outdoors or in the garage. If that's not possible, brush the dog while he's standing on a sheet so you can simply gather it up and throw it in the washing machine when you're through.

Shorthaired Dogs

A good brush for most shorthaired dogs is a rubber curry brush that fits over the hand. You can find a good selection of curry brushes and hound mitts at well-stocked pet-supply stores. Also get a steel comb with wide and narrow teeth to help remove tangles. Breeds that shed heavily may also benefit from the use of a shedding blade, shedding comb, or wire slicker brush, but if you choose to use these, be aware of the following points:

* These tools have sharp edges or teeth that remove excess coat. Use them once or twice a week, after first brushing with the curry.

* You should move a shedding blade over the body in the direction that the hair grows. If you bear down too hard, the sharp edges may injure your dog.

* Using a shedding blade on the legs or other areas where the hair is thin and fine, such as the belly, can break the skin and cause injury.

* Avoid using shedding tools too often or you'll remove too much coat, leaving your dog with a flaky or scaly appearance.

Longhaired Dogs

Longhaired dogs are prone to mats and tangles, but daily brushing helps keep these problems under control. The following chart tells you what tools you need for your longhaired dogs and what they will accomplish.

Tool	What It Does
Pin brush	A pin brush, which has long metal "pins" coming out of the pad, helps lift out loose hair and skin debris without removing a lot of undercoat. When you're finished grooming, you can use the pin brush to fluff the coat by brushing against the direction that the hair grows.
Shedding or de-matting comb	Use this to break up matted sections before combing them out completely.
Wire slicker brush	Use the slicker brush to gently remove knots and tangles.
Shedding blade	When your dog is "blowing," or shedding coat, a shedding blade comes in handy to remove all that excess hair.
Bristle brush	The bristle brush brings out shine once the other tools have done their work.

Run the pin brush through the coat in the direction that the hair grows. Check for mats behind the ears, on the backs of the legs, in the groin area, and on the tail. If necessary, use the shedding comb to remove any mats. Work at it slowly, starting at the bottom of the mat and working toward the skin, being careful not to pull your dog's hair. Try to avoid cutting the mat, because that will simply make the area more prone to matting. Spending just a few minutes each day to remove tangles before they get bad will save you time in the long run, and it will also save your dog pain.

Wirehaired Dogs

Besides the usual brushes and combs, you'll need a few additional tools to groom a wirehaired dog. Review the following checklist to see what you need for your wirehaired pup:

- [ ] TRIMMING AND THINNING SCISSORS

- [ ] ONE OR TWO STRIPPING KNIVES

- [ ] A SET OF CLIPPERS

- [ ] CORNSTARCH OR GROOMING CHALK

You can keep a wire coat in good condition with weekly brushing. Use a pin brush or a natural bristle brush. First, brush in the opposite direction of the hair growth, then brush in the direction of hair growth. Care for leg and facial hair with a wire slicker brush. The slicker brush is also useful for removing undercoat.

To maintain its correct hard texture, a wire coat must also be stripped twice a year. Stripping is a technique done to remove dead hair and shape the coat. You can strip the coat by hand or with a special tool called a stripping knife. Your breeder or a groomer can show you how to strip the coat and advise you on the types of stripping knives and scissors to purchase. If stripping seems like too much work, you can simply have the coat clipped, but be aware that this will soften the texture and color of the hair. Wirehaired show dogs are never clipped, and if you want your dog to maintain the proper wire look, stripping is the way to go.

Wirehaired breeds also have facial hair—eyebrows and a beard—that must be trimmed and shaped. Before you start, wash the furnishings (as facial hair is known) and work in some cornstarch or grooming chalk. Comb the hair forward and use scissors to trim as desired. For a pet, you'll just want your dog to have a neat appearance, but if you plan to show your dog, you'll need to get detailed advice from your breeder or another person experienced in the breed to achieve the correct look.

Hairless Dogs

If you have a hairless dog, you don't need to worry about grooming at all, right? Wrong! These breeds have special needs, as their delicate skin is prone to acne and sunburn. Different hairless breeds have different skin types, so your dog's breeder is the best person to advise you about appropriate skin care. However, here are some basic facts and tips:

* Hairless dogs with good skin—smooth and clear with tiny pores—rarely need baths. Hairless dogs with larger pores or oily skin that's prone to acne may need baths with a mild shampoo every one or two weeks to keep their skin in good condition and oil production at a minimum.

* Contrary to what you may have heard, hairless breeds perspire only through their paw pads, just like other dogs.

* If your dog is prone to acne, use a medicated shampoo or acne medication recommended by your veterinarian or breeder. Often, acne clears up after adolescence, just as it does in humans.

* After a bath, you may need to moisturize the skin to keep it soft and supple. This is especially important if you live in a dry climate. You can use gentle products made for human use. Coat oil made for dogs can also help keep a hairless dog's furnishings—the hair on the head, feet, and tail—in good condition. Carefully brush the hair with a pin brush.

* Hairless breeds sunburn easily. Keep them indoors during the heat of the day, and make sure they're protected with sunscreen if they do go outside. Choose a sunscreen that's safe if your dog licks it off, or purchase one that's specially made for dogs. Look for it at pet-supply stores, your veterinarian's clinic, or at online pet-supply sites.

Method	What to Do
Offer food	If there's one thing that can capture a dog's attention, it's food. For some, this is the trick that makes nail clipping at home possible. Simply distract the dog by feeding bite-sized treats one at a time while you clip the nails out of view.
Do a few at a time	Perhaps your dog can sit still long enough to have a few nails clipped, but all four feet is just too much to ask. In this situation, try doing a few nails per day over the course of a week. This will give your dog breaks in between clippings, but you'll still have all the nails done within a reasonable time.
Grind away	Though clippers are most common, some people choose to use a nail grinder for this task. A grinder will make more noise, but it grinds away the nail instead of snipping it off. It may seem strange, but some dogs prefer the steady grinding sensation to the sudden clip. You can also use a manual grinder (similar to an emery board), but this could take more time than you have to spare.
Leave it to the vet	If your dog struggles too much for you to even attempt nail clipping at home, bring him to the vet. Vets are well trained to handle fussy dogs, and having the vet do the dirty work will free you up to comfort your pup.

The Everything Dog Owner's Organizer

Nail Trimming

The first key to nail trimming success is getting your pup used to having his feet handled. Once this is achieved, nail maintenance should not be traumatic, as carefully removing the tips of the nails will not hurt. However, some dogs are finicky about their feet, and some just don't like the feeling of being held in one spot for that long. In these cases, there are other methods to try (see chart on page 52).

If you've never clipped a dog's nails before, be sure to have your veterinarian or breeder demonstrate how to do it correctly and safely. Styptic powder will also come in handy in case you accidentally cut the quick and cause bleeding.

Cleaning Eyes and Ears

Dogs with long, hanging ears, such as spaniels or retrievers, often develop ear infections. The inside of the ears is warm and moist, an ideal home for bacteria to flourish. To prevent problems, keep the ears clean and dry, especially if your dog loves to go swimming. Pups should also be comfortable with you carefully wiping any discharge from their eyes with a damp cloth and checking their ears. This daily routine, followed with a small treat, will make it much easier for you and your veterinarian if your dog ever has a problem. When you clean the eyes and ears, also check for the following:

- **REDNESS IN OR AROUND THE EYES:** This could indicate irritation or injury.

- **SQUINTING OR WATERY EYES:** This could indicate irritation or injury.

- **FOUL ODOR COMING FROM THE EARS:** This could indicate infection. Take him to the vet right away.

Notes and Observations

Use the following spaces to mark down any problems or changes you encounter when bathing or grooming your dog. Also mark down the date you first noticed these issues. During your next visits to the vet and groomer, bring out this list and discuss your concerns, ask questions, and record possible solutions.

HEAD
- Eyes: _____
- Ears: _____
- Muzzle and nose: _____
- Teeth and gums: _____

BODY
- Back: _____
- Belly: _____

❧ Tail: _____

❧ Coat: _____

LEGS AND FEET

❧ Legs: _____

❧ Pads: _____

❧ Toenails: _____

Use the following lines to write down anything you learn in your discussions with your vet and groomer about your dog's grooming needs.

_____

_____

_____

_____

_____

_____

_____

_____

_____

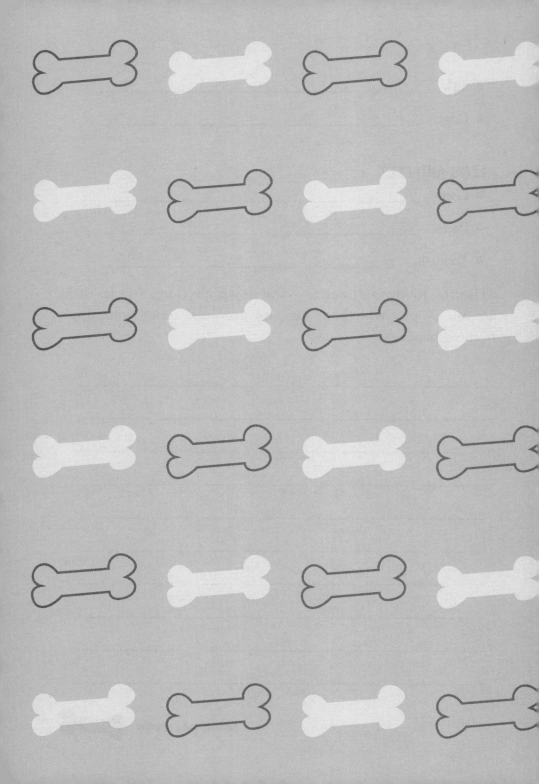

chapter 5

Nutrition

Food Basics

All dog food labels must contain five pieces of information: the guaranteed analysis, which tells you the minimum and maximum levels of protein and fat the food contains; the nutritional adequacy statement; the ingredients; the feeding guidelines; and the manufacturer's name and address.

Somewhere on the label there should also be a statement of which life stage the product is made for: growth/lactation (puppies or pregnant/lactating females), maintenance (adults), or all life stages (any dog). The Association of American Feed Control Officials (AAFCO) recognizes only two life-stage profiles, growth/lactation and maintenance. Therefore, a food labeled "seniors" or "large breeds" simply meets the AAFCO requirements for adult dogs.

Dog Food Ingredients

An ingredient list is useful for telling you what's in a food, but it can't tell you the quality of the ingredients. However, there are some tricks to reading a label that will help you be a more informed dog food shopper.

First, ingredients are listed by weight, in descending order. While some dog foods may list meat as the first ingredient, if you look farther down the label you may notice that it also lists a particular grain in several different forms, such as wheat flour, flakes, middlings, or bran. Individually, each form of wheat might make up only a small part of the food, but together they may outweigh the meat it contains. Look for a food that contains a balance of meat and grain proteins.

Secondly, dietary protein contains ten essential amino acids that dogs cannot make on their own. The best dog foods have meat protein as the first ingredient. Protein from meat is higher in quality than protein from grains. Forms of meat protein include meat by-products and meat meals, which is meat that's been heat-processed to remove fat and water.

Take a few notes on the dog food you're currently feeding to your dog:

🐾 Essential ingredients that are lacking:

_____

🐾 Mysterious ingredients to learn about:

_____

Different Types of Food

Dogs are individuals, and different dogs do better on different types of foods. Whether you choose a canned, dry, or other type of dog food depends not only on your dog's needs, but also on your budget, what's most convenient for you, and how you feel about certain types of ingredients. Consider all these factors when you're choosing a food. Each type has advantages and disadvantages.

Food Type	Pros	Cons
Canned	Long shelf life until opened. Dogs enjoy the taste.	Can be expensive. Must be refrigerated after opening.
Dry kibble	Easy to scoop, measure, and serve. Inexpensive.	Many dogs find canned food tastier than dry.
Frozen	Flash freezing requires no artificial preservatives.	Must be thawed before serving.
Dehydrated	Prepared at a temperature low enough to preserve the vitamins, minerals, and other nutrients yet high enough to kill any bacteria. Just mix with warm water and serve.	Leftover rehydrated food must be refrigerated.
Homemade	Can be tailored to your dog's specific dietary needs and tastes.	Time intensive. Difficult to prepare a nutritionally complete meal at home.

In addition to the different conditions of food, there are also other types to consider. For instance, dog food is often categorized as popular, premium (which may include organic), or generic. One of the main differences between these three types is digestibility, which is the proportion of nutrients in a food available for the body to absorb and use. Digestibility is determined over a period of days by measuring the amount of food a dog takes in and the amount of fecal matter he produces, which is then analyzed in a laboratory to see how much is nutrient waste and how much is normal metabolic waste.

- **POPULAR FOODS:** These are the national or regional brands that you find in grocery stores. One disadvantage of these foods is that their formulas can vary from batch to batch, depending on the cost and availability of ingredients, which can cause stomach upset in some dogs. Popular foods aren't as digestible as premium foods, but they're of better quality than generic foods.

- **PREMIUM FOODS:** Found primarily in pet supply stores, these contain high-quality ingredients that provide good to excellent digestibility and are prepared according to fixed formulas. Some premium foods may contain organic or human-grade ingredients. Premium foods are expensive, but because of their higher digestibility you can feed less of a premium food, which brings down the cost per serving.

- **ORGANIC FOODS:** Premium foods are often labeled as organic, which refers to the way plants were grown or animals were raised (usually without the use of pesticides or fertilizers or only certain types of pesticides or fertilizers). Currently, the U.S. Department of Agriculture (USDA) does not have any rules governing the labeling of organic foods for people or pets, although this will probably change in the future.

☙ **GENERIC FOODS:** These foods are attractively priced, but that's because they use poor-quality ingredients to keep costs down. Ingredients can vary from batch to batch depending on price and availability. The nutritional quality of generic foods is rarely confirmed through AAFCO feeding tests, and some may not even carry a nutritional adequacy statement. In fact, because of the low level of digestibility, it's necessary to feed a lot more of a generic food, so the savings are illusory.

Use the following lines to take notes on your dog's reactions to different types of foods. Just be sure that you don't switch foods too quickly. This could wreak havoc on your pup's digestive system, creating a seemingly negative reaction to the food.

_____

_____

_____

_____

_____

_____

_____

Treats and Snacks

It's pretty safe to say that dogs love treats. And what a dog considers a treat can range from pieces of his regular kibble to commercial treats to bits of hot dog, cheese, fruits, or vegetables. Dogs are pretty much happy with anything you give them to eat, but not all treats are created equal. Here are some tips on treating your dog healthily:

- **KEEP TREATS SPECIAL.** Offer them only as a reward; don't just hand them out indiscriminately.

- **LIMIT TREATS.** They should make up no more than 10 percent of your dog's daily food intake.

- **READ TREAT LABELS.** Avoid those that are high in sugar and fat, or give them only in small amounts.

- **VARY TREATS.** Dogs like crunchy things, sweet things, and savory things. Offer bits of chopped apple, banana, or carrots, fresh or frozen berries, cubes of cheese or hot dogs, baked liver bits, and biscuits.

- **TAILOR THE TREAT TO THE OCCASION.** Use tiny bite-size treats for training, larger biscuits or long-lasting chews for going into the crate or doing something else that doesn't require instant follow-up.

- **KNOW WHAT'S NOT A TREAT.** Chocolate, grapes, alcohol, and onions are all toxic to dogs.

Dog treats are held to the same FDA and state labeling requirements as dog foods, but they're not required to be nutritionally complete. Biscuits are the exception to this rule, unless they're specifically labeled as a "snack" or "treat." Rawhide chews, pig ears, and similar items made from animal materials or parts are considered food by the FDA, but unless they claim some nutritional value, such as "high protein," their manufacturers aren't required to follow AAFCO pet food regulations. A treat product is required to list the manufacturer's address and to have an ingredient list if it contains more than one ingredient.

As you try out different types and brands of treats, keep track of your dog's reaction—both physically and in terms of enjoyment. Does digestion go smoothly or does she get an upset stomach? Does she slide the treat around with her nose for ten minutes before eating it, or does she scarf it right up?

Type or Brand of Treat	Any physical reaction?	Yum or Yuck?

Puppy Nutrition

A puppy has different nutritional needs than an adult dog. Growing requires extra amounts of certain vitamins and minerals, and these must be present in the correct ratios. Growing pups need different amounts of protein and energy sources as well. Too much can be as bad as too little! Your pup's food should say "Balanced and complete for all life stages" or be specifically labeled as a "puppy food." The best foods will not only have a complete nutritional analysis on the label but will state somewhere that they were tested with feeding trials. A laboratory analysis is not a substitute for actually testing a diet by feeding it to dogs.

Before you bring your new puppy home, ask your breeder what food he has been feeding. You should try to use that food at least for the first week or so to make the new home transition easy for your pup. If you intend to switch foods, do so gradually over a week or so. Resist the temptation to ply your new family member with exotic and wonderful goodies.

Determining Mature Weight

With many pure breeds, you'll have a fairly accurate idea of your dog's eventual adult weight even when he is just a pup. Mixed-breed puppies adopted from animal shelters, however, don't come with papers detailing their parents' breed or size. But there's a rule of thumb that will get you in the ballpark. Take the puppy's weight at eight weeks, multiply by four or five, and the result will give you an estimate of her adult size. This is only an estimate, but it can help you figure out whether you need to feed a food geared for a large or small breed. Use the following table to estimate your pup's adult weight.

Weight at 8 Weeks of Age	Estimated Adult Weight
5 pounds	20-25 pounds
10 pounds	40-50 pounds
15 pounds	60-75 pounds
20 pounds	80-100 pounds

How Much to Feed and When

Your veterinarian and your breeder can help you work out the best diet for your pup. Discuss what amount to feed and how often, as well as what foods are best. The following guidelines can give you a head start:

* Most pups do best with three meals a day until four months or so, and then stay on two meals daily for the rest of their lives.

* Very small toy-breed puppies may need extra snacks to keep them growing well.

* Specific meal times are preferred to feeding free choice (leaving a bowl of food out for your dog to graze on). With set meals, you know right away if your pup isn't feeling well. You can easily keep track of just how much your pup is eating, and it helps with housetraining on a schedule.

🐾 Puppies should have access to fresh water almost all the time. However, you may want to limit water shortly before bedtime or an hour or two before heading out on a long car trip.

Puppy Treats

Let's face it—as well as her regular food, your puppy will be getting treats and chew items. Treats can help train your pup and help develop your close bond. Remember that if you use a lot of treats in training, you may need to cut back on your pup's mealtime amounts. Most puppies are happy to use their regular food as training treats, but if you want special treats, talk to your veterinarian. Don't forget that pieces of chopped apples or carrots are good and healthy treats for your dog. They're low-calorie and good for her teeth!

Adult Dog Nutrition

Your dog's nutritional needs depend in large part on his breed and size. Some dogs reach physical maturity much more rapidly than others, with large-breed puppies taking the longest to mature. In general, the growth of any dog starts to slow at about six months of age, but the following table offers some more detailed information.

Size of Dog	Growth	Food Requirements
Small dogs	Those that weigh less than 20 pounds, have a higher metabolic rate than large-breed dogs, so they burn energy more quickly.	They need a nutrient-dense diet that gives them a lot of nutrition in a small amount of food. Their stomachs just aren't that big relative to their needs.
Medium-size dogs	At nine months to one year of age, their skeleton will be full size, or almost there.	Most of these breeds can start eating adult dog food around nine months to one year of age.
Large and giant-breed dogs	These breeds don't reach full physical maturity until they're two and sometimes even three years old.	These dogs should eat a large-breed puppy diet or a diet customized by your veterinarian until they're two years old. Some manufacturers add ingredients such as glucosamine and chondroitin to diets for large-breed puppies and adult dogs. These nutrients are believed to help improve joint cartilage, and they remain stable in foods for long periods.

The exceptions to the rule are the small but stocky breeds, such as pugs, which are prone to skeletal problems if they grow too quickly. They can start eating an adult food as early as five months of age.

Switching Foods

When it's time to switch your dog from puppy food to adult food, or if you simply want to change brands, always do so gradually. Dogs have sensitive stomachs, and a rapid dietary change can bring on vomiting or diarrhea. Begin by adding small amounts of the new food to your dog's regular food over a period of five to ten days. The more different the foods are from one another, the more gradual the change should be.

For instance, if you're switching from Brand A puppy food to Brand B adult food, the change should go more slowly than if you're changing within the same line of food; say, from Brand X puppy food to Brand X adult food. Also change gradually if you're switching from dry food to canned food or vice versa. Allow plenty of time for the dog's gastrointestinal system to fully adapt to the new diet.

Nutrition for Older Dogs

A healthy older dog can continue to eat the same diet as long as she maintains a good weight and her coat and skin remain in good condition. If you notice some symptoms of aging, there may be something you can do. The following list of problems common to older dogs also offers possible solutions.

Sign or Symptom	Reason	What to Do
Weight gain	Like people, dogs tend to become less active with age, so they need fewer calories to maintain an appropriate weight.	Because their aging body is less able to metabolize protein efficiently, they need a food with reduced levels of fat and calories, but high levels of protein. Added fiber can also help reduce the calorie count, while still giving your dog the feeling of a full belly.
Thinning coat	Like aging humans, dogs also suffer from thinning hair. Follicles are just not as productive anymore.	Certain nutritional supplements may help, such as essential fatty acids, vitamin E, and zinc.
Dry, itchy skin	As dogs age, their skin glands produce less oil, increasing the chances of dry skin.	Certain nutritional supplements may help, such as essential fatty acids, vitamin E, and zinc. Always check with your veterinarian before adding any supplements to be sure your dog's diet will still be balanced, especially in puppies.

Checking thyroid levels is important in older dogs with weight gain or coat changes as well. As a general rule, always ask your veterinarian for a recommendation when it comes to physical changes in your adult dog.

A Feeding Schedule

Dogs do best when they eat regular meals at specific times every day because they're less likely to eat too much. Consistent meal times also help with potty training. Physiologically, dogs have the urge to go after they eat, so by scheduling meals and taking your dog out immediately afterward, you can accustom him to eliminating at certain times. Finally, dogs are creatures of habit. They like knowing that meals will appear at certain times every day.

Adult dogs do well on two meals a day, morning and evening. Puppies typically eat three or four meals a day. That's because they're growing, so they need more nutrients than adult dogs. If you aren't able to provide midday meals, don't worry. Simply divide the amount of food the puppy needs for the day into two meals, and he'll do just fine. The exception might be a small toy-breed puppy. These little dogs sometimes need a snack between meals to keep their energy levels up. You can do this for any dog by filling a treat ball or cube with kibble. Your dog will occupy himself by trying to get the kibble out, and he'll get the snack he needs even if you're not home to feed him.

Write It Down

Decide with your family what time of day you will feed your dog and create a weekly schedule with times of day and the names of the family member who will do the feeding. Don't forget to include more frequent feedings or snack times for puppies and toy breeds.

Here's a sample of what your schedule might look like:

SUNDAY	9:00 A.M.: Biscuit (Danny) 5:00 P.M.: Dinner (Beth)
MONDAY	8:00 A.M.: Biscuit (Mom) 5:00 P.M.: Dinner (Dad)
TUESDAY	8:00 A.M.: Biscuit (Danny) 5:00 P.M.: Dinner (Beth)
WEDNESDAY	8:00 A.M.: Biscuit (Mom) 5:00 P.M.: Dinner (Dad)
THURSDAY	8:00 A.M.: Biscuit (Danny) 5:00 P.M.: Dinner (Beth)
FRIDAY	8:00 A.M.: Biscuit (Mom) 5:00 P.M.: Dinner (Dad)
SATURDAY	9:00 A.M.: Biscuit (Danny) 5:00 P.M.: Dinner (Beth)

SUNDAY	
MONDAY	
TUESDAY	
WEDNESDAY	
THURSDAY	
FRIDAY	
SATURDAY	

Helpful Tips

Choosing food, feeding times, and amounts to feed can be tricky at first, but once you develop a routine, you won't even think about it. The following tips will help you get organized and remember key points when it comes to feeding your pup:

* **MEASURE THE FOOD.** Don't just fill his dish until it's full. Use a measuring cup or a kitchen scale so you feed an appropriate amount. If you're using a measuring cup, give a level cup instead of a heaping one.

* **SLOW HIM DOWN.** If your dog "inhales" his food, spread it out on a flat surface such as a cookie sheet (use one with raised edges to keep the food inside it). This forces him to slow down and eat at a more moderate pace.

* **KEEP IT CLEAN.** Wash your dog's dishes regularly. Choose dishes that are dishwasher-safe, and keep extras on hand so you have one set to use while the other is in the dishwasher.

* **TEACH PATIENCE.** Teach your dog to wait politely while you prepare his food. Dogs love mealtime, and they'll whirl around in circles or jump up on you while you fix their food to show their appreciation. Channel this energy by asking your dog to sit while you prepare his food. Put the bowl down, tell him to stay, and then give him permission to eat by saying "Okay!" or "Chow!"

All of these tricks make mealtime more pleasant for both you and your dog.

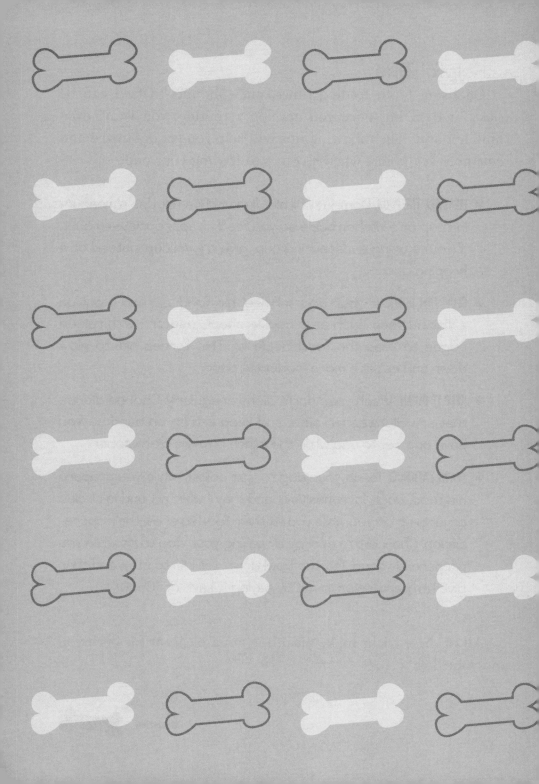

chapter 6

Veterinary Care

The Veterinary Visit

Your veterinarian is your number-one partner in caring for your dog. If you're looking for one, get recommendations from shelter staff, breeders, and friends with dogs. If possible, go and check out the clinic and staff yourself. You want a clean facility that provides emergency coverage, with friendly staff members who welcome your questions, and a reputation for good medical care.

An annual veterinary exam (plus visits as needed for illness or injury) is the best way to keep your dog healthy from nose to tail. Although you know your dog best, your veterinarian will often see or feel things that you might miss. Your veterinarian also has specialized instruments to fully examine your dog.

During the annual exam, you and your veterinarian should discuss the following aspects of your dog's health:

* Physical condition

* Vaccination status

* Parasite control

* Dental health

* Nutrition

* Behavior

When you visit the vet, bring this organizer with you. Refer to any notes you may have taken that discuss changes in your dog's physical condition or behavior. Using a pencil, check off any of the following that you'd like to discuss and provide details in the spaces given. The dates and specifics can help the veterinarian figure out what's going on. After the visit, erase the marks and reuse for the next vet visit.

☐ DISCHARGE, REDNESS OR ITCHING AFFECTING THE EYES

_____

_____

_____

☐ DISCHARGE, REDNESS OR ITCHING AFFECTING THE EARS

_____

_____

☐ **SKIN PROBLEMS**

_____

_____

_____

☐ **CHANGES IN COAT CONDITION**

_____

_____

_____

☐ **CHANGES IN EATING HABITS OR FOOD TOLERANCE**

_____

_____

_____

☐ **CHANGES IN EXERCISE TOLERANCE**

_____

_____

_____

☐ **CHANGES IN GENERAL BEHAVIOR**

_____

_____

_____

During the exam, the veterinarian will listen to your dog's heart and respiration rate; examine the eyes and ears; palpate (examine by touch) the body to check the condition of the internal organs and make sure there are no unusual lumps or bumps; and test your dog's joint and muscle condition by moving his legs to check his range of motion. You will also want to bring in a stool sample so the veterinarian can examine it for the presence of parasites.

Once the physical exam is complete, you and the veterinarian can discuss how your dog is doing and whether any changes should be made in his care. This is also a good time to mention any behavioral problems you might be having with your dog. If your veterinarian doesn't find an underlying medical cause for the behavior, she should be able to refer you to a veterinary behaviorist or experienced trainer who can help.

Vaccinations

When puppies are born, they become temporarily protected from disease by nursing from their mother. The first milk she produces, called colostrum, contains maternal antibodies that protect the pup during the first weeks of life. Dogs can also acquire what is called natural, or active, immunity if they become ill with—and survive—a particular infectious disease. Viral immunities formed from natural exposure usually last for a long time, though bacterial immunities do not.

Vaccination provides what is known as acquired immunity. A vaccine is a substance that, when injected, provides immunity against infectious diseases caused by bacteria, viruses, and other organisms. It does this by challenging the body with modified disease organisms, provoking the immune system to form antibodies against those particular organisms. Vaccinations don't necessarily provide lifelong immunity and must be repeated at certain intervals.

Core and Non-core Vaccines

The decision to vaccinate a dog against a particular disease depends partly on the dog's age, breed, and potential exposure to the disease. It also has a lot to do with the distribution and virulence of the particular disease. Certain canine diseases are widely distributed, highly contagious among dogs, and serious or sometimes even fatal. Once a dog has acquired them, no treatment other than supportive therapy can help. The vaccines against these diseases are referred to as core vaccines, meaning that they are recommended for all puppies and dogs. These diseases are canine parvovirus, canine distemper virus, canine adenovirus, and rabies. In the following list, check off which vaccinations your dog has received, and write down the date of the vaccination in the space provided.

☐ CANINE PARVOVIRUS

_____

_____

_____

☐ CANINE DISTEMPER VIRUS

_____

_____

_____

☐ CANINE ADENOVIRUS

_____

_____

_____

☐ RABIES

_____

_____

_____

Other vaccines are considered optional. When deciding whether to give them, you and your veterinarian should take into account the geographic distribution of the disease and your dog's risk of exposure. For instance, if your beagle is a show dog that never sets foot in field or forest, she's not at very high risk for Lyme disease. The non-core vaccines are those against canine parainfluenza virus, Bordetella bronchiseptica (also known as kennel cough), leptospirosis, giardiasis, Lyme disease, coronavirus, distemper, and the measles. Again, check off those vaccines your dog has already received, and write down the date of vaccination in the space provided.

☐ CANINE PARAINFLUENZA VIRUS VACCINATION

_____

_____

_____

☐ BORDETELLA BRONCHISEPTICA VACCINATION

_____

_____

_____

☐ **LEPTOSPIROSIS VACCINATION**

_____

_____

_____

☐ **GIARDIASIS VACCINATION**

_____

_____

_____

☐ **LYME DISEASE VACCINATION**

_____

_____

_____

☐ **CORONAVIRUS VACCINATION**

_____

_____

_____

☐ **DISTEMPER/MEASLES COMBINATION**

_____

_____

_____

According to the vaccination guidelines of the Veterinary Medical Teaching Hospital at the University of California at Davis, vaccination with these non-core vaccines is generally less effective in protecting against disease than vaccination with the core vaccines. Some of these diseases are not common in many areas of the country, so there's no reason to give them unless your dog is at risk. Your veterinarian can tell you which are necessary in your area.

Vaccination Progress

Puppies receive vaccinations against parvovirus, distemper, and adenovirus-2 (canine hepatitis) at six to eight weeks of age, again at nine to eleven weeks, and then a final series at twelve to sixteen weeks. Keep track of your pup's vaccination progress using the following lists. Check off the different progress points, and write the dates of vaccination and details in the spaces provided.

PARVOVIRUS

☐ SIX TO EIGHT WEEKS

_____

_____

_____

☐ NINE TO ELEVEN WEEKS

_____

_____

_____

☐ TWELVE TO SIXTEEN WEEKS

_____

_____

_____

DISTEMPER

☐ SIX TO EIGHT WEEKS

_____

_____

_____

☐ NINE TO ELEVEN WEEKS

_____

_____

_____

☐ TWELVE TO SIXTEEN WEEKS

_____

_____

_____

ADENOVIRUS-2 (CANINE HEPATITIS)
☐ SIX TO EIGHT WEEKS

_____

_____

_____

☐ NINE TO ELEVEN WEEKS

_____

_____

_____

_____

_____

_____

A dog older than four months of age with an unknown vaccination history needs one dose of vaccine against these diseases. After a booster shot at one year, most authorities recommend revaccination every three years.

The first rabies vaccination is generally given at sixteen weeks (four months) of age. Boosters are usually given at three-year intervals, although a few states require annual rabies vaccination. Adult dogs with an unknown vaccination history need a rabies vaccination as well.

Important Details

Most vaccine labels recommend that the vaccine be administered annually. No scientific studies support this frequency of vaccination, however, and there's good evidence that the effects of vaccination last for much longer. While your dog still needs an annual exam, there's usually no reason for her to receive annual vaccinations. Frequent vaccinations may be advisable under some circumstances, so be sure to speak to your vet. For example, the Bordetella vaccine (which is given nasally) does not appear to last very long. If you kennel your dog frequently, or if she often comes in contact with strange dogs at shows or dog parks, she may need this vaccine up to twice a year.

Here are some other important details and tips to remember when it comes to vaccinations:

* Reactions to vaccines are rare, but they can occur. Keep a close eye on your dog for the first few hours after she receives vaccinations to make sure she doesn't develop any serious allergic reactions.

* Keep Benadryl (diphenhydramine) on hand, and ask your veterinarian how much to give in case your dog develops hives, swelling, redness, or itchiness in response to a vaccination. The vaccines that are most commonly linked to reactions are those for leptospirosis, rabies, and parvovirus.

* Too-frequent vaccination has been associated with autoimmune diseases such as autoimmune hemolytic anemia, and many veterinarians and dog owners are concerned that overvaccination can have other ill effects that are not yet known or understood.

* Before you schedule your dog for revaccination against distemper, parvovirus, or adenovirus-2, you may want to have her titer levels tested. A titer is the concentration of an antibody in blood serum. If these levels are still high, she probably doesn't need to be revaccinated.

Medications

No matter how hard you work to keep your dog healthy, she's sure to need medication at some time in her life. To make sure medication is effective, you'll need to know how to give it, how much to give, and how long to continue giving it. Each issue is essential in ensuring your dog's return to good health. Here are some main points to remember regarding medications:

* Your dog's medication may come in the form of a pill, liquid, or drops for the eyes or ears. Before you leave the veterinarian's office, make sure you understand when to start giving the medication, whether it should be given with food or on an empty stomach, and how often you should give it each day.

* You should inform the veterinarian of any herbal or holistic remedies or other medications your dog is taking. They might interfere with the effectiveness of the prescribed medication.

* It is important to give your dog the full course of medication, even if she seems to be better after the first few days. Her body needs to build up a certain amount of the drug in the bloodstream for it to be fully effective. That's also why drugs need to be given at specific intervals, such as every eight hours.

Use the following table to keep track of your dog's prescribed medications, dosages, and methods of administration. Later, you can always refer to this table if you forget the dosage or need to tell the vet which medications your dog is on.

Medication	Single Dose	Dosage per Day	Method of Administration

How to Give Pills

Giving pills to a dog can be tricky, but there are a couple different ways to get it done. Check off the method that works best with your dog, and write down any notes you'd like to remember for the next time you give the pills:

❧ **HIDE THE PILLS INSIDE SOMETHING TASTY.** Peanut butter, cream cheese, and canned dog food are all excellent "carriers" for pills. But before you follow this plan, ask your veterinarian if it's okay to do this. Some medications shouldn't be mixed with certain foods. For instance, tetracycline shouldn't be given with dairy products like cream cheese.

_____

_____

_____

☙ **GIVE THE PILLS BY HAND.** If you have a dog that eats the yummy coating and spits out the pill, or if the pill should be given on an empty stomach, you'll need to give it by hand. Holding the pill in your dominant hand, use the other hand to hold the dog's mouth open. Place the pill toward the back of the tongue, close the mouth, and stroke the dog's throat to encourage swallowing. When you think she has swallowed, do a finger sweep inside her mouth to make sure it went down.

_____

_____

_____

☙ **INVESTIGATE OTHER OPTIONS.** If your dog balks at taking a pill, ask the vet if there's another way to give it. Some drugs can be made into syrups that are applied to the gums so the medication is absorbed through the mucous membranes. Others can be compounded into something tasty, such as peanut butter, to make them more palatable.

_____

_____

_____

Though it might work for children, you don't want to crush pills and sprinkle them on your dog's food. Crushed pills can have a bitter flavor that make her reluctant to eat, and you won't have any way of knowing if she gets all the medication.

How to Give Liquids

Most liquid medications come with a dropper for dispensing them. If they don't, you can use a plastic syringe (the kind without a needle), as long as it has the proper measurement markings. Follow these steps for administration:

1. Fill the dropper or syringe with the appropriate amount of medication, and hold it in your dominant hand, using your other hand to open the dog's mouth.
2. Place the dropper in the mouth, aiming it at the cheek pouch, and pinch the lips closed.
3. Slowly release the plunger and continue holding the lips closed until the dog swallows.
4. Always end with a reward, such as a tasty treat (if food can safely follow the medication) or a favorite toy.

Eye and Ear Drops and Ointment

Administer eye drops straight from the bottle. Tilting the dog's head upward, hold the bottle in your dominant hand and squeeze the prescribed number of drops into the eye. Try not to touch the eye with the applicator tip. To apply an ointment to the eye, hold the head still with one hand, and pull the lower eyelid downward. Using your dominant hand, squeeze a small amount of ointment onto the eyelid, then release the eyelid and gently rub the surface of the closed eye to distribute the ointment over the eyeball. Again, be careful not to poke the dog in the eye with the applicator. It may help to have someone else hold her head for you.

Ear medications often need to go deep into the ear, so they usually come in a tube or bottle with a long, narrow applicator. Place the applicator inside the ear and dispense the appropriate amount. Be sure you have a firm grasp on your dog's head while you do this. Before she can shake his head and send the medication flying, fold the ear over and gently massage it to make sure the medication is thoroughly distributed.

Spay/Neuter Surgery

If you don't plan to breed your dog—and you shouldn't, unless you have a superb example of the breed whose characteristics would improve the gene pool—you have two options for preventing puppies:

- **ABSTINENCE:** You'll need to make sure your female is securely confined during estrus (heat). This is trickier than it sounds, because she will make every effort to escape in search of male companionship—and every male for miles around will be trying to get to her as well. And, of course, you'll need to make sure your male doesn't have any opportunity to impregnate the local females.

- **SPAY OR NEUTER SURGERY:** Spay surgery, or ovariohysterectomy, is the removal of the female's uterus and ovaries. Neutering is the removal of the male's testicles, to prevent the production of sperm.

Traditionally, spay/neuter surgery is performed just at or before the onset of puberty, though it can be safely performed as early as six weeks of age. It is often done this early on puppies adopted from animal shelters. Animals this young don't require as much anesthesia as older puppies or adult dogs, and they recover rapidly from surgery. Many veterinarians like to schedule spay/neuter surgery at four or five months of age, when puppy vaccinations have been completed.

Besides its main purpose of birth control, spay/neuter surgery has health benefits:

- Females that are spayed before their first estrus cycle are much less likely to develop breast cancer later in life than females spayed after one or more cycles. They are also spared the risk of developing ovarian cysts or uterine infections.

☙ Neutered males have no risk of testicular cancer and are at reduced risk for prostate enlargement and perianal adenomas, which are tumors of glands found around the anus.

☙ Dogs that are spayed or neutered are also more likely to get along better with other dogs and less likely to roam (unless they are scent hounds, in which case they are genetically programmed to follow tantalizing scents).

Preparation

Before surgery, the veterinarian may recommend running a blood panel to make sure your dog is in good health. If your dog is young and has no known health problems, the only blood work will mostly likely be a simple test for blood urea nitrogen (BUN) levels, total blood protein, and a hematocrit, which is the ratio of packed red blood cells to whole blood. An aging dog or one that's not in tip-top health may need more extensive blood work. Check off the blood tests as your dog has them performed and write the results in the spaces provided.

☙ BUN levels

_____

_____

_____

❧ Hematocrit

_____

_____

_____

❧ Other test

_____

_____

_____

❧ Other test

_____

_____

_____

Before the surgery, ask the veterinarian a few questions about the procedure. Discuss whether or not the following steps will be taken, check off the boxes for those that will, and write down any important notes:

☐ DURING SURGERY, THE VETERINARIAN OR A STAFF MEMBER WILL MONITOR YOUR DOG'S BREATHING AND HEART RATE.

_____

_____

_____

☐ THE VETERINARIAN WILL TAKE THE PRECAUTION OF PLACING AN IV CATHETER IN A VEIN. (THIS SAFETY MEASURE ALLOWS DRUGS TO BE INJECTED QUICKLY IN THE EVENT OF AN EMERGENCY.)

_____

_____

_____

☐ THE VETERINARIAN WILL PROVIDE THE DOG WITH PAIN-RELIEF DRUGS BEFORE, DURING, AND AFTER SURGERY. (THE USE OF THESE DRUGS ENSURES THAT YOUR DOG SUFFERS AS LITTLE PAIN AS POSSIBLE AND RECOVERS MORE QUICKLY.)

_____

_____

_____

Recovery

During the first few days after surgery, your dog may be tired and a little sore, even with pain medication. Other dogs are as frisky as ever, running around and bouncing off the walls. Whether your dog feels well or not, it's important to keep him as still as possible. Rest will help the incision heal more quickly. Here are a few important tips to keep in mind for the recovery phase:

❧ You can limit activity by keeping your dog on leash or confining him to a crate.

❧ You can keep your dog from licking or biting at his stitches by using what's known as an Elizabethan collar. This plastic, cone-shaped collar (which resembles a lampshade) fits around your dog's neck, preventing him from reaching the sutured area. Dogs hate wearing these and will shake their heads in vain attempts to remove them. Luckily, many dogs never bother their sutures.

❧ Some swelling at the incision site is normal, especially if the veterinarian uses absorbable sutures. Depending on the type of suture, swelling may last for six to eight weeks. This swelling may be more noticeable on a dog with thin, delicate skin.

❧ You should visit the vet if redness, obvious inflammation, or any discharge (other than a little pinkish stuff the first day or so) occurs at the incision site. These are signs of possible infection.

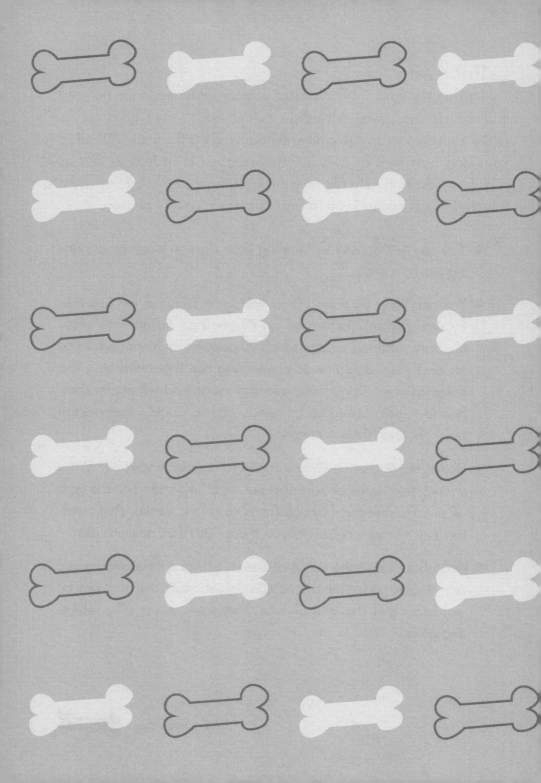

chapter 7

Your Dog's Health

Signs of Illness

Any behavior or physical quality that is out of the ordinary for your dog should always be taken under scrutiny. It could be a simple scratch from walking through the woods, or just a runny nose, but it could also be an early sign of illness. The following list contains some of the more common problems you might notice in your dog.

❧ **BLEEDING FROM ANY ORIFICE:** A bloody drip from the vulva of a spayed female or from the penis of a male may indicate a bladder infection. Blood from the vulva of an unspayed female dog who is not in her heat cycle could indicate an overgrowth of the uterine lining or a uterine infection—both potentially life-threatening. Blood in stool can be black due to a problem such as a stomach ulcer, or bright red from a bleeding problem in the intestines.

- **DIFFICULTY BREATHING:** A dog in pain often has quick, shallow breathing. Any abdominal problem that puts pressure on the diaphragm can cause respiratory difficulty as well. A dog that has been hit by a car or had other trauma might have broken ribs or what is called a pneumothorax (free air in the chest, putting pressure on the lungs), which requires immediate veterinary care.

- **EXCESSIVE DRINKING:** Diarrhea and vomiting dehydrate your dog. Fever or mild heat stroke can stimulate dogs to drink more than usual, as can bladder infections and mild kidney problems. More serious problems like kidney failure can also lead to increased drinking and urinating. With diabetes mellitus, either the pancreas doesn't produce enough insulin or the insulin present isn't working properly to remove extra glucose from the blood. A diabetic dog therefore drinks more water to flush out the extra glucose. Female dogs with pyometra (uterine infections) will often be very thirsty, and dogs with increased calcium in the blood secondary to cancer are also very thirsty.

- **UNEXPLAINED WEIGHT LOSS:** Weight loss occurs in one of two ways—either insufficient calories are being taken in, or extra calories are being burned. Diabetes mellitus is one example of a disease in which a dog may have a good (if not voracious) appetite but still lose weight. This disease affects the production of insulin so the dog can't use all the calories consumed.

- **COUGHING AND SNEEZING:** A sneeze with a thick or discolored discharge should be looked into. Dogs can snort up grass or bugs, or they may develop cancerous growths that block nasal passages and cause repeated sneezing. Coughing may be the result of something simple like inhaling water, or it could be a sign of a serious problem, such as cancer or pneumonia. Heart problems that allow fluid to build up in the lungs may be accompanied by a cough as well. Some of the worst sounding coughs are actually caused by a respiratory virus known as kennel cough, whose symptoms are treatable.

* **DISCHARGE FROM EYES, EARS, AND NOSE:** Your dog's eyes, ears, and nose are all sensitive areas with plenty of specialized nerve endings to help with seeing, hearing, and sense of smell. Any discharges from these areas may interfere with your dog's keen senses and may indicate a deeper problem.

* **SCRATCHING AND BITING THE SKIN:** A dog that is itching, rubbing, and scratching is an uncomfortable dog. Along with the discomfort, the pruritus (itchiness) may be a sign of underlying problems, such as allergies. The skin itself is an important first-line barrier against bacteria and parasites. Skin that is scratched with tiny cuts is ripe ground for infections. Anything more than an occasional scratch or rub (such as many dogs do right after they eat) is worth investigating.

* **LISTLESSNESS, LAMENESS, AND COLLAPSING:** If your dog is normally bouncing around, begging someone to throw a toy or go for a walk, you should be concerned if one day he is just lying quietly in the kitchen. Any time your dog holds up a paw, is walking awkwardly, or is reluctant to move, you should investigate the cause. Lethargy, lameness, and collapse can all be signs of serious problems.

- 🐾 **SWELLING OR BLOATING:** A healthy dog normally has a trim figure with a waist that can be clearly seen when you look from above and a tuck-up right before the hind legs when you look from the side. A sudden increase in width is a definite cause for alarm. Bloat, or gastrointestinal volvulus, is a life-threatening condition that happens when a dog's stomach has twisted.

- 🐾 **DIARRHEA AND VOMITING:** Vomiting and diarrhea may come together as a pair of gastrointestinal problems, or they may show up separately. These problems can be mild and minor or serious and life threatening.

Using the following chart, mark down any of these problems you've noticed in your dog, the date you discovered the problems, and detailed notes on your dog's condition. These will be useful when you bring your dog to the vet.

Problem	Date Discovered	Details of Condition

Once you've gone to the vet, write down the diagnosis and treatment for each problem. These notes will become a useful part of your dog's medical history. (See chart on following page.)

Problem	Veterinary Diagnosis	Treatment

The Everything Dog Owner's Organizer

Recognizing Pain

Pain is often difficult to recognize and interpret in dogs, but in no way does that imply they don't feel it. Whether pain is short-term or long-term, it can make your dog's life very unpleasant if it's not managed properly. Pain may certainly have a protective role in minimizing injury and preventing further damage, but unrelieved pain can make a dog's condition worse and has no beneficial effects. Any time you believe your dog is in pain, ask your veterinarian what can be done to help.

The response to pain can be involuntary or voluntary. For instance, when a groomer's nail clippers cut into the quick, the painfully sensitive blood vessel that feeds the nail, the dog reflexively jerks his paw back. That's an involuntary response. A voluntary response is based on experience. A dog who's had his nails clipped too short in the past remembers the pain and jerks his paw back before the clippers even touch the nail.

The sensation of pain can originate in the skin, bones, joints, muscles, or internal organs. Each causes a different type of pain:

- **CUTANEOUS PAIN:** This type of pain is caused by injury to the skin or superficial tissues. Minor cuts, burns, and lacerations are examples of cutaneous pain.

- **SOMATIC PAIN:** A broken bone or sprained joint produces somatic pain, which originates from ligaments, tendons, bones, blood vessels, and nerves.

❧ **VISCERAL PAIN:** Nociceptors located within body organs or body cavities produce visceral pain, such as a stomachache.

Signs of Pain

Recognizing and finding the source of pain in dogs is a challenge. Dogs can't say where it hurts or how much it hurts, so you and your veterinarian must rely on your knowledge and observations of your dog's normal behavior.

The early signs of pain are subtle. They might include eating less, failing to greet you at the door when you come home from work, or not wanting to be groomed when normally that's a pleasurable experience. More obvious signs of pain include limping, reluctance to move, squinting or pawing at the eyes, crying out or whining when touched, or even snapping when touched. Any unexplained abnormality in your dog's routine behavior or activity level is significant and warrants a visit to the veterinarian. Common signs of pain you should watch for include the following. Check off those you notice in your dog and mark down any specifics in the space provided.

☐ CHANGES IN PERSONALITY OR ATTITUDE, SUCH AS A NORMALLY QUIET AND DOCILE DOG BECOMING AGGRESSIVE OR AN AGGRESSIVE DOG BECOMING QUIET

_____

_____

_____

_____

☐ ABNORMAL VOCALIZATIONS, SUCH AS WHINING OR WHIMPERING, ESPECIALLY WHEN A PAINFUL AREA IS TOUCHED OR THE DOG IS FORCED TO MOVE

_____

_____

_____

_____

☐ LICKING, BITING, SCRATCHING, OR SHAKING OF ONE AREA

_____

_____

_____

_____

☐ PILOERECTION, A REFLEX OF THE MUSCLES AT THE BASE OF THE HAIR SHAFTS THAT CAUSES THE HAIR TO STAND ON END

_____

_____

_____

_____

☐ CHANGES IN POSTURE OR MOVEMENT, SUCH AS LIMPING, HOLDING A PAW UP, OR TENS-
ING THE ABDOMINAL AND BACK MUSCLES TO PRODUCE A TUCKED-UP APPEARANCE

_____

_____

_____

_____

☐ CHANGES IN ACTIVITY LEVEL, INCLUDING RESTLESSNESS, PACING, LETHARGY,
OR RELUCTANCE TO MOVE

_____

_____

_____

_____

☐ LOSS OF APPETITE

_____

_____

_____

_____

☐ **CHANGES IN FACIAL EXPRESSION, SUCH AS DULL EYES OR PINNED EARS**

_____

_____

_____

_____

☐ **CHANGES IN BOWEL MOVEMENTS OR URINATION, SUCH AS STRAINING**

_____

_____

_____

_____

Your veterinarian will check your dog's heart rate, respiratory rate, and body temperature. All of these tend to increase in the presence of pain. The veterinarian may check a blood sample for elevations in glucose, corticosteroid, and catecholamine concentrations.

Diagnosing Pain

To find the source of the pain, your veterinarian will probably begin by palpating your dog's body, examining it by hand to check the condition of the organs and search for painful lumps or bumps. He may put pressure on the trigger points along the spine and check the range of motion of the legs by extending and flexing the joints to look for signs of discomfort. Once he knows where the pain is, your veterinarian can try to figure out what's causing it and how to treat it.

When there isn't an obvious cause for pain, such as a surgical wound, for instance, or a broken bone, sophisticated diagnostic techniques can help. These include analysis of the cerebral spinal fluid, radiographs of the spine using dye (myelography), measurements of the electrical activity in the muscles (electromyography), and brain imaging with computed tomography (CT) or magnetic resonance imaging (MRI) scans.

Managing Pain

Pain management is important for any condition that interferes with your dog's normal activity, appetite, interaction with you, and ability to have a good day. How pain is managed depends on the type and cause of the pain. Some pain can be cured, while other types of pain can only be managed. In any case, preventing and relieving pain is an important goal that you and your veterinarian can work toward together.

The first thing to realize is that complete elimination of pain isn't necessarily possible or desirable. The main goal is to help your dog cope with pain so she doesn't suffer. Successful pain management allows a dog to continue to engage in normal activities, such as eating, sleeping, moving around, and interacting with people or other animals. Factors your veterinarian will take into account in approaching pain relief are your dog's breed, age, health status, personality, the drugs and techniques available, and the type, cause, and degree of pain.

Traditional Therapies

Medication is probably the first form of pain relief that most people think of, and most veterinarians use drugs with pain-relieving properties as the first line of defense against pain. The following list contains different types of drugs you might come across as a dog owner:

- ❧ **OPIOIDS** usually have the effects of dulling the senses, relieving pain, or inducing sleep. Opioid patches placed on a dog's skin can provide long-lasting and steady pain relief, unlike shorter-acting medications that can wear off before the next dose is given.

- ❧ **ANALGESICS** include local anesthetics, which numb only a particular area.

- ❧ **NONSTEROIDAL ANTI-INFLAMMATORY DRUGS** (NSAIDs) are often used to treat the chronic pain of arthritis or cancer. NSAIDs don't directly eliminate pain, but they can decrease it by treating inflammation. Several NSAIDs have been developed specifically for use in dogs, including carprofen, etodolac, meloxicam, and deracoxib.

- ❧ **SEDATIVES** work to decrease anxiety and can enhance the effectiveness of analgesic drugs, but they don't necessarily relieve pain in and of themselves. Never assume that a sedative or

tranquilizer by itself will be enough to relieve your dog's pain. Acepromazine, or "ace," is a commonly used sedative that does not provide much in the way of pain relief.

Dogs process drugs differently than people. Never give your dog any kind of pain-relief medication without first checking with your veterinarian. Tylenol and ibuprofen, for example, are toxic to dogs even in very small amounts.

Remember that your veterinarian is tailoring the type of drug, dose, and frequency of administration to your dog's individual needs. Just because your neighbor's dog is getting good pain relief from a certain medication doesn't mean that your dog will respond the same way. The dose and duration of effect of analgesic drugs varies greatly from dog to dog. Your veterinarian may also choose to use a combination of analgesic drugs from different drug classes to achieve the best pain relief and reduce the risk of side effects. As your dog's needs change, your veterinarian may modify the dose or frequency of administration. He may also require periodic blood work to make sure the drug isn't affecting liver function, which is a common side effect.

Nonmedical Pain Management

Effective pain management goes beyond drugs. Keeping your dog comfortable will also help her feel better more quickly. Here are some tips to help you do this:

🐾 If your dog is recovering at home, place her bed in a quiet, well-ventilated area.

- Take steps to limit any stress on your dog. She may love your kids and the neighbors' kids, but she's not up to dealing with them right now. Keep visits short and quiet.

- Your dog needs to eat well to recover, so diet is important right now. She may be in so much pain she doesn't feel like eating, but she needs nutrition in order to heal. Tempt your dog's appetite with canned food. If that doesn't work, try warming her food in the microwave. Test it with your finger before giving it to her to make sure there aren't any hot spots.

- Weight loss is another aspect of diet that can help relieve your dog's pain, especially if she suffers from an orthopedic condition such as arthritis or hip dysplasia. While there's no cure for osteoarthritis or hip dysplasia, a weight-reduction plan may delay the need for surgery. This is especially important for large-breed dogs.

Alternative Therapies for Pain Relief

So many people have found pain relief through alternative therapies such as acupuncture and chiropractic methods that they want their dogs to experience the same benefits. These types of alternative and complementary therapies are no longer unusual for animals; many traditionally trained veterinarians now offer their clients a full range of services by joining forces with or making referrals to practitioners that offer these treatments. Among the therapies that may benefit dogs are the following:

- 🐾 Acupuncture

- 🐾 Chiropractic therapy

- 🐾 Magnetic field therapy

- 🐾 Massage

- 🐾 Nutraceuticals

Few studies have been done to prove the effectiveness of these treatments. Much of what's known has been extrapolated from studies in humans. Nonetheless, many dog owners believe alternative therapies have made a difference in their pets' quality of life. Because not much is known about how or why certain treatments or techniques work in animals, always go to an experienced practitioner. Just because something is natural doesn't mean it's harmless.

External Parasites

In dogs, the external parasite category includes fleas, ticks, mites, and lice. These creatures must be associated with a dog or other animal for at least part of their lifetime. Not only do they drain nutrients from dogs, they cause a wide variety of health problems and may even transmit diseases. Your goal as a responsible dog owner should be to keep your dog as parasite-free as possible for a long, healthy life.

Fleas

Fleas can leap many times their own height, run very swiftly, and have become resistant to many anti-flea medications. They not only cause healthy dogs to itch but can stimulate severe allergic reactions and can also carry other parasites and diseases. Tapeworms can be transmitted by the bite of a flea. A heavy load of fleas on a small puppy can cause serious anemia. Fleas will even enjoy a meal of your blood if they get the chance, along with any furry pets such as rabbits and cats.

prevention

Preventing flea infestations is easier than getting rid of them once they have moved in. This means the best plan for fighting fleas is to take action before you see evidence of them. Check off the following points as you accomplish them, and write notes next to each:

☐ WHEN WARM WEATHER APPROACHES, START THINKING ABOUT FLEA CONTROL, WHICH IS OFTEN COMBINED WITH TICK CONTROL.

_____

_____

_____

- [ ] ASK YOUR VET ABOUT NEW MEDICATIONS THAT ACT AS FLEA BIRTH CONTROL BY INTERFERING WITH THE DEVELOPMENT OF THE FLEA'S PROTECTIVE CHITIN COVERING.

_____

_____

_____

- [ ] LOOK INTO INSECT GROWTH REGULATORS, WHICH STOP ANY FLEAS THAT GET ON YOUR DOG FROM SUCCESSFULLY REPRODUCING.

_____

_____

_____

- [ ] RESEARCH DRUGS THAT ACT TO KILL FLEAS. MANY OF THESE MEDICATIONS NOW COME IN TOPICAL FORMS THAT CAN BE APPLIED TO YOUR DOG ONCE MONTHLY. PYRETHRINS (FROM CHRYSANTHEMUMS) ARE FOUND IN MANY FLEA-CONTROL PRODUCTS.

_____

_____

_____

- [ ] REMEMBER THAT FLEA-CONTROL PRODUCTS THAT ARE SAFE FOR USE ON YOUR DOG ARE OFTEN NOT SAFE FOR USE OTHER PETS. WHILE YOU NEED TO TREAT ALL THE FURRY ANIMALS IN YOUR HOUSEHOLD IF YOU HAVE A FLEA

INFESTATION. REALIZE THAT YOU MAY NEED SPECIAL MEDICATIONS FOR EACH SPECIES.

_____

_____

_____

finding fleas

Most of the fleas we see on our dogs are actually the cat flea—Ctenocephalides felis. Once adult fleas find a suitable host, they feed by taking blood meals. Then the females lay eggs, which may stick to the hair of your dog or fall off in the areas where she sleeps, lies, or walks in your house. Larvae hatch and go into a pupa where the adult fleas will develop. Adult fleas can remain safely in the pupa for long periods of time (months) until hosts show up. They can detect movement, warm temperatures, and even carbon dioxide, so they definitely know when a living being passes close by.

Follow these steps to see if your dog has fleas:

1. Part the hair and look for tiny running bodies. It may be easiest to roll the dog over and look in the relatively hairless area of the groin.
2. If you see or feel dark grit in your dog's coat, take some off and put it on a white paper towel.

3. Add a drop of water to the grit on the paper towel. If it dissolves and turns red, you know it is flea feces–the red is from the blood meals.

fighting fleas

Fighting fleas requires a concerted effort. *All* your pets need to be treated—even the cat—along with any dogs that may not show any itching. You need to get rid of the adult fleas, stop reproduction, and with any luck prevent new fleas from joining the family. Check off the following points as you complete them:

☐ GIVE YOUR DOG A FLEA BATH USING FLEA SHAMPOO.

☐ FOLLOW THE FLEA BATH WITH A DIP, SPRAY, POWDER, COLLAR, OR TOPICAL TREATMENT TO DETER NEW FLEAS OR EVEN KILL THEM IF THEY TRY TO RETURN.

☐ THOROUGHLY CLEAN ALL RUGS, AS WELL AS AREAS ALONG WALLS AND BEHIND DOORS.

☐ CAREFULLY FOLLOWING INSTRUCTIONS, SET OFF FLEA BOMBS TO CATCH ANY FLEAS THAT ARE LEFT IN THE HOUSE.

☐ OUTSIDE, TRY PLANTING CHRYSANTHEMUMS, SPREADING BORAX OR DIATOMACEOUS EARTH, AND DISCOURAGING RODENTS (WHO MAY SERVE AS HOSTS) FROM LIVING NEAR YOUR HOME.

Mark down the dates and details of any flea encounters your dog has had. This information will be useful to the veterinarian if he finds any problems with your dog.

Date of Flea Encounter	Details

Ticks

Ticks are tough arachnids (eight-legged creatures) that not only eat blood meals but may carry many serious, life-threatening diseases. They come in a variety of sizes (all small, though), and the primary species vary from region to region. Ticks can be differentiated from fleas in that they are rounder and they either walk or are firmly fixed to your dog's body. Most are brown, but some, such as deer ticks, are very small and whitish in color. Female ticks get very large after a blood meal and their color changes from brown to a grayish shade.

prevention

As always, the best plan is to prevent tick infestations to begin with. Do the following and take notes for each point:

☐ LOOK INTO THE TOPICAL AGENTS AND COLLARS USED FOR FLEA CONTROL, AS MANY OF THESE WILL ALSO WORK AGAINST TICKS.

_____

_____

_____

_____

☐ WHEN SEARCHING FOR REMEDIES, FIND SOMETHING THAT WILL KILL THE TICKS ALMOST IMMEDIATELY—THEY MUST FEED FOR TWENTY-FOUR TO FORTY-EIGHT HOURS TO PASS ON MOST DISEASES. BETTER YET, SOME PRODUCTS WILL REPEL THEM FROM YOUR DOG TO BEGIN WITH.

_____

_____

_____

_____

☐ IF YOU LIVE IN AN AREA WITH TICKS OR PLAN TO TRAVEL WHERE TICKS ARE COMMON, DISCUSS WITH YOUR VETERINARIAN THE BEST AND SAFEST METHOD TO PROTECT YOUR DOG.

_____

_____

_____

_____

finding ticks

The ticks most often found on dogs are the dog ticks, Derma-
centor variabilis and Rhipicephalus sangineus, and the deer tick
Ixodes scapularis. These ticks go through four life stages:

1. Female ticks lay eggs after they engorge with a blood meal.
   The eggs may be deposited in cracks and crevices or on the
   ground.
2. The eggs hatch into larvae that climb up on grass, hitch a
   ride on a host, and take a big blood meal themselves.
3. The third stage is a nymph, which follows another cycle of
   hitching a ride on a host and taking a blood meal.
4. The final stage–the adult.

Unfortunately ticks aren't only a threat for the blood-sucking
damage they do. Many ticks can carry one or more deadly diseases. The list includes the following:

* Lyme disease

* Canine ehrlichiosis

- Canine babesiosis

- Rocky Mountain spotted fever (no longer confined to the Rocky Mountain area)

These diseases may show up as problems in the blood with immunity deficits or anemia; swollen, painful joints; rashes; fevers; and damage to the heart. These sidekicks have the potential to kill your dog. You are susceptible to many of these diseases as well, if a tick feeds off you.

Fighting Ticks

Like fighting fleas, fighting ticks is a two-stage battle—removal and prevention. If you find ticks on your dog, they need to be carefully removed. There are special tweezers made to remove them, and you should wear gloves to prevent infection. Do not use a lighted match or pour gasoline on the tick. It doesn't work and is dangerous to your dog. If the head is left in your dog's skin, a localized infection may result. Your veterinarian can help you treat those spots.

Mark down the dates and details of any tick encounters your dog has had. This information will be useful to the veterinarian if he finds any problems with your dog.

Date of Tick Encounter	Details

Mites

Mites are a group of small parasites that may attack dogs. There are three main mites that might be found on dogs: the ear mite, Otodectes cynotis; the sarcoptic mange mite, Sarcoptes scabiei; and the demodectic or red mange mite, Demodex canis. Skin problems caused by mites are often referred to as mange. Demodex is not contagious, though ear mites and sarcoptic mites are. They will spread among dogs, from cats to dogs, and (rarely) even to people! If one pet in your household is found to have mites, it is a good idea to check them all carefully.

- **EAR MITES:** These tend to be found in dogs that live with cats. You might notice dark, coffee-ground type buildup in your dog's ears, and she may be scratching a bit.

- **SARCOPTIC MANGE:** These mites burrow into the top layers of the skin, where even a few of them can stimulate a very strong itch response. Dogs with sarcoptic mange can barely walk, as they keep stopping to scratch. With all the scratching, they have open skin areas, which are then in danger of infection. Sarcoptic mange mites are contagious, and dogs with these parasites often have picked them up from local wildlife, including foxes and squirrels.

- **DEMODEX:** This tiny mite can be found in normal dogs. Most dogs get along quite well with their demodectic mites and have no problems. Unfortunately, some dogs have immune problems that are either temporary, as may be seen in puppies or debilitated dogs, or permanent from immune defects. In these dogs, the mites overgrow and cause skin reactions. A few red spots on a puppy may be treated topically or may clear up with no treatment. Dogs that have more than five spots or large areas of reddened, sore skin have generalized Demodex.

- **CHEYLETIELLA:** Cheyletiella is a short-lived mite most often seen on puppies. It shows up as a line of dandruff down their backs. This mite is not usually a serious threat to your dog's health and can be treated by medicated baths.

Mark down the dates and details of any mite encounters your dog has had. This information will be useful to the veterinarian if he finds any problems with your dog.

Date of Mite Encounter	Details

mite diagnosis and treatment

Your veterinarian can diagnose an ear mite infestation by examining a swab of the discharge under a microscope. Most cases can be treated with topical ear medications, though severe cases may need a parasiticide.

Skin scrapes are used to diagnose cases of mange. Your veterinarian will choose a couple itchy areas of skin and pucker it to scratch a sharp blade across the top. The thin skin layers are then examined under a microscope.

Diagnosing sarcoptic mange can be tricky. Skin scrapes are the best method, but it can be hard to find mites. If your veterinarian suspects sarcoptic mange, he may start treatment even with a negative skin scrape. Sarcoptic mange is often treated with a combination of drugs along with baths or dips. Any related infections must also be treated, and your veterinarian will try to make your dog comfortable and relieve some of the itching.

Demodex is usually easily diagnosed by a skin scraping. Dogs with generalized Demodex will need serious treatment, often with both drugs and dips combined. Since this condition is associated with a genetic defect, dogs that suffer from it should be spayed or neutered and not bred.

Lice

Like mites, lice are also parasites that attack dogs via their skin, though they aren't very common in dogs. Lice come in two main types—biting and sucking. Biting lice tend to be smaller and can move quickly. Lice tend to be host-specific, which means they rarely move from people to dogs or vice versa. Neither type is very common in dogs. Puppies may sometimes have lice from a dirty environment and may spread to them from their mother. A large number of lice could make a puppy anemic, but normally the effects are just poor coats and nits or eggs attached to hair shafts. In most cases, medicated baths or dips will take care of this parasite.

Internal Parasites

The most common internal parasites in dogs are roundworms (especially the Toxocara species), hookworms (primarily Ancylostoma), and whipworms (Oxyuris). Tapeworms are not as common but they are just as worrisome. These parasites live in the intestines and drain vital nutrients that growing puppies need.

* **ROUNDWORMS:** These parasites can infect puppies before they are born and can also be transmitted via the dam's milk. Adult dogs get roundworms by accidentally ingesting eggs deposited on the ground. The immature larvae migrate through your dog's body and can cause damage to the liver and lungs. Puppies with roundworms often show a bloated abdomen, dull coat, diarrhea, and possibly intestinal blockages. Adult dogs develop some resistance, but even they can show the effects of roundworms.

* **HOOKWORMS:** These are smaller than roundworms but have a set of mouth hooks that dig into the intestines and drain nutrients and blood. Again, puppies can be infected in utero or via their dam's milk. Hookworms can be ingested and can also penetrate the skin, and they cause skin lesions in people as they migrate through the body. Hookworms can actually kill a puppy by making it severely anemic. Dogs with hookworms will show anemia, possibly bloody diarrhea, weight loss, and poor coats.

* **WHIPWORMS:** Not as prevalent as roundworms or hookworms, these are small intestinal parasites with a whip-like, tapering tail. The eggs need to be ingested to complete their life cycle, but they can survive in the ground for long periods of time. Whipworms cause diarrhea, often with mucus and blood. Dogs with whipworms may defecate frequently and strain to do so. A large number of whipworms can be a serious drain on an adult dog, let alone a puppy. Whipworms are resistant to treatment, so repeated treatments may be necessary.

* **TAPEWORMS:** The most common tapeworms are Dipylidium caninum and Taenia pisiformis. These two have different life cycles, and differentiating them is important for treating your dog and preventing future cases of tapeworm infestation. Dipylidium use fleas as their intermediate host. Dogs that have fleas often accidentally eat one while grooming and scratching. Taenia use rodents as their intermediate host, and dogs that hunt mice or rabbits can pick them up while hunting if they eat their prey. Tapeworms are often discovered when you see what appear to be dried rice segments around your dog's tail and rectum.

A fecal sample from your dog is often the best way to diagnose intestinal parasites. You need to bring a small amount of stool (about a tablespoon, preferably fresh) to your veterinarian. This will be mixed with a special salt solution and either run through a centrifuge or allowed to sit. The final solution will be examined under a microscope to see if it contains eggs passed by adult parasites living inside your dog.

Mark down the dates and details of any worm problems your dog has had. This information will be useful to the veterinarian if he finds any problems with your dog.

Date of Worm Problem	Details

Protozoan Problems

Protozoal parasites are small single-cell organisms that can't exist very well outside their given host or a specialized environment. Many of the common protozoa we may find in our dogs can also affect people. Good hygiene is very important in dealing with these and other parasites:

- **GIARDIA:** This protozoal parasite is quite hardy and can exist for long periods of time in a wet environment. Streams and ponds are its favorite sites. Drinking infected water may lead to severe diarrhea, sometimes with blood or mucus. The cysts are then passed into the feces and may contaminate other bodies of water. There are treatments for giardia, but it can be difficult to diagnose. This parasite can be spread to people as well, so you and your dog should both avoid drinking water from streams or ponds in areas where this parasite is known to exist. There is now a vaccine for dogs in epidemic areas.

- **COCCIDIA:** There are many species, but virtually all work the same way. Dogs that live in a less-than-clean environment, especially puppies, may ingest cysts through contaminated food or fecal material. Dogs with coccidia may show diarrhea, sometimes with blood. In puppies this can be a debilitating disease. People are resistant, but kennel areas still need to be kept immaculately clean to prevent puppies picking up this protozoan.

The best way to diagnose protozoal infections is with a fresh fecal sample. In this case, your veterinarian will take a small sample directly from your dog's rectum. The sample will be mixed with saline and examined under a microscope for protozoa actively moving around. A regular fecal test would kill the protozoa and make them virtually impossible to detect.

Mark down the dates and details of any protozoal problems your dog has had. This information will be a useful part of your dog's medical history.

Date of Protozoal Problems	Details

Treating Intestinal Parasites

As always, one of the best treatments for disease problems is prevention. Keeping your dog's play area clean, picking up after your dog on walks, yearly or even twice-yearly fecal checks, and helping your dog to stay in the best condition possible all reduce parasite problems. Still, it is possible for your dog to pick up parasites just by walking where a dog deposited eggs days before. So even the best-cared-for dog may have parasites at some time.

Here is a list of some traditional treatments and prevention methods:

☐ YEARLY OR EVEN TWICE-YEARLY FECAL CHECKS ARE A QUICK, EASY, AND RELATIVELY INEXPENSIVE WAY TO MAKE SURE YOUR DOG NEVER GETS A SERIOUS PARASITE LOAD.

☐ ALWAYS PICK UP AFTER YOUR DOG, AND ENCOURAGE OTHERS TO DO SO FOR THEIR DOGS AS WELL.

☐ IF YOU ARE ADDING A NEW DOG TO YOUR FAMILY, DO A FECAL CHECK AS SOON AS POSSIBLE SO YOU DON'T CONTAMINATE YOUR YARD WITH PARASITE EGGS OR LARVAE.

☐ SOME SAFE MEDICATIONS THAT WILL KILL THE PARASITES AND LEAVE YOUR DOG IN GOOD HEALTH INCLUDE PYRANTEL PAMOATE, IVERMECTIN, AND FEBENDAZOLE. DIFFERENT MEDICATIONS ARE USED FOR DIFFERENT PARASITES, AND SOME PARASITES MAY DEVELOP DRUG RESISTANCE, REQUIRING YOU TO TRY A SECOND, DIFFERENT MEDICATION.

☐ IF YOU SEE WORMS OR SUSPECT A PARASITE PROBLEM, CHECK WITH YOUR VETERINARIAN. MANY OVER-THE-COUNTER DEWORMERS ARE NOT VERY EFFECTIVE.

☐ CERTAIN PARASITES, SUCH AS WHIPWORMS, MAY REQUIRE REPEATED TREATMENTS ON A SET SCHEDULE TO TOTALLY CLEAR YOUR DOG.

☐ DO A FOLLOW-UP FECAL CHECK AFTER FINISHING A COURSE OF TREATMENT TO BE SURE IT WAS EFFECTIVE.

There are also some herbal and homeopathic medications that are believed to be effective for dewormings. Remember, just because something is natural or organic does *not* mean it is safe! Do not try any of these remedies without consulting a veterinarian experienced in their use. Black walnut is often touted for dewormings, along with garlic, but used incorrectly both of these could be toxic to your dog (as could many traditional dewormers if used incorrectly). Follow-up fecal checks are important to determine that treatment was successful.

Heartworms

Heartworms, Dirofilaria immitis, are potentially life-threatening parasites in dogs. Adult heartworms live and thrive in the heart and pulmonary arteries of dogs. Some may also be in the lungs in large blood vessels. These are long-lived parasites, some living as long as five years! During this time, if there are both males and females present, they produce many tiny young, called microfilaria. The microfilaria get into the bloodstream and are picked up when a mosquito bites your dog. These microfilaria develop in the mosquito and then move to its mouth so that they can be injected into another dog when the mosquito feeds. In other words, this parasite can only be spread from dog to dog with the help of a mosquito.

Dogs with a mild case of heartworm will cough, lose some of their stamina, and may be weak or short of breath. The worms block the blood supply of fresh oxygen to other tissues, including the lungs, heart, kidneys, and liver. By the time these clinical signs show up, some of the damage is irreparable. Dogs may die from a heavy load of heartworms.

prevention

Certainly, the ideal situation is to prevent heartworms from infecting your dog to begin with. There are numerous preventive medications. These range from daily pills to monthly medications. Work is also being done on even longer-range products. Some of these medications require that your dog test negative for heartworm first, as a rapid die-off of the parasites could cause shock reactions. These products may be effective against some of the intestinal parasites your dog is susceptible to as well. Some practitioners use black walnut herbal preparations and homeopathic remedies along with twice-yearly blood tests to catch early infections. Check with your veterinarian about a safe product for your dog. Some breeds are sensitive to ivermectin, a common ingredient in heartworm preventives, and should use other medications.

Keep track of any preventive heartworm medications you've used with your dog.

Heartworm Medication	Start Date	Dosage/Administration

diagnosis

Heartworm diagnosis may involve multiple specialized tests. There are a few simple and easy tests your veterinarian can run right in the clinic. The first is to check a blood sample for antigens. This test picks up protein in the blood shed by adult heartworms. This test will pick up infections early—with luck before the adults are even reproducing. This test specifically looks for proteins from female worms. If your dog only has one or two worms, there may not be enough antigen to detect. A second test screens a blood sample for actual microfilaria. While microfilaria found in a blood sample are almost always from heartworms, they do need to be clearly identified before any treatment is started.

Keep track of your dog's blood test results in the following space:

Type of Test	Date of Test	Result

Your veterinarian may also want to do X rays or even an echo-cardiogram (special ultrasound of the heart) to look for worms or the damage they cause. Enlargement of the heart and the large blood vessels that go to the lungs are highly suggestive of heart-worm infection. A complete blood panel may be done before any treatment is started to see if your dog already has liver or kidney damage.

treatment

Dogs that are diagnosed with heartworm infections will need treatments to kill both the adults and the microfilaria. Currently the only approved treatment for the adults is an organic arsenic compound—obviously a drug to be used with care, as you want to poison the worms but not your dog! This medication requires intravenous administration and your dog may need to be hospitalized for care and observation. Dogs must be kept quiet after this treatment. While the adult heartworms are now dead, your dog's body must absorb the remains and keep any pieces from shedding off and causing trouble. Some veterinarians have been successful using ivermectin at higher than preventive dosages as well.

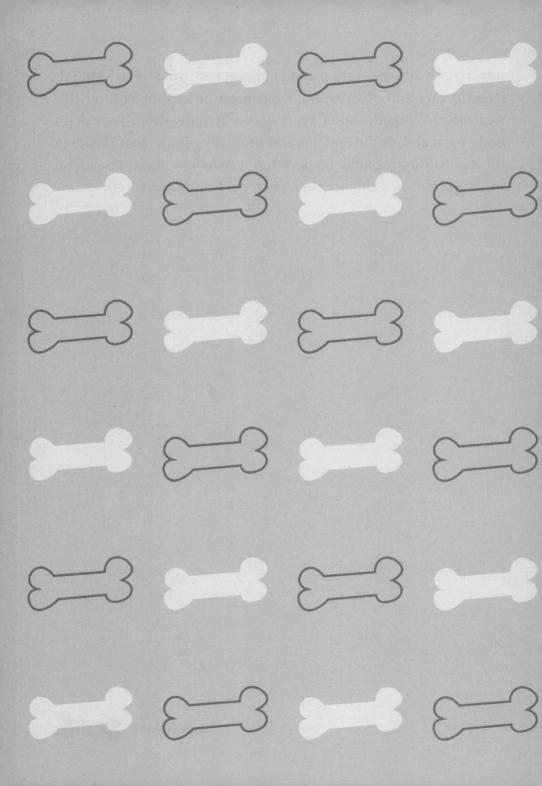

PART 3

Exercise, Socialization, and Training

Exercise and Play

Socializing Your Dog

Basic and Obedience Training

part three
Exercise,
Socialization,
and Training

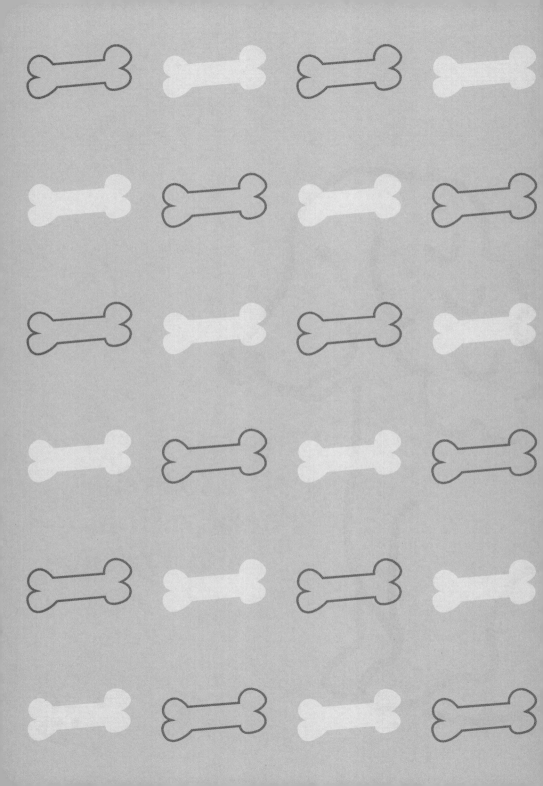

chapter 8

Exercise and Play

Exercise Guidelines

From the tiniest toy breeds all the way up to the giants of the canine world, all dogs need exercise and play to keep them healthy and mentally sharp. A dog that simply lies around all the time becomes dull and depressed. Dogs are active animals that need and enjoy interaction with people and other dogs. Daily walks, indoor and outdoor play, and training sessions all contribute to your dog's physical health and mental well being.

Here are some guidelines to keep in mind as you develop an exercise plan for your dog:

* ❧ The amount of exercise your dog needs depends on her age, breed, and individual activity level. Your goal is to keep your dog from becoming soft and flabby. Every dog should have firm muscles and a defined waist that you can see when you look down at her from above.

* Dogs of all breeds need lots of free play-running loose in an enclosed yard or chasing balls, for instance. This helps build strong muscles and bones. Puppies also need to practice walking nicely on leash so they don't pull and choke themselves.

* Rambunctious pups should be prevented from jumping on and off furniture and running on hard surfaces, as both can injure their growing bones and joints.

* The most active adult dogs tend to be examples of the sporting, working, terrier, and herding breeds. Expect to give them at least thirty minutes to an hour of good, hard exercise every day. Jogging and dog sports such as agility and flyball are great ways to give these dogs the action they need.

Create a Schedule

Since your dog needs exercise every day, your family needs to decide who will take on this responsibility. Perhaps one child will walk the dog after school three days a week, while another child will do it for the remaining four days of the week. Or maybe someone is awake early in the mornings and can take the dog for a quick run before leaving for work. Whatever schedule you choose, make sure it is relatively consistent and offers your dog sufficient exercise every day.

Use the following chart to map out a weekly schedule for your dog's exercise. Once it's complete, make a copy and post it on the refrigerator or on a bulletin board where everyone in the family can refer to it.

Day of the Week	Time of Day	Activity	Person Responsible
Sunday			
Monday			
Tuesday			
Wednesday			
Thursday			
Friday			
Saturday			

Sports and Exercise Programs

When people start a new sport or exercise program, they are usually advised to check with their doctor to make sure they're in good physical condition. You should do the same for your dog if you're planning to get her started in one of the many dog sports or even if you just want a canine jogging or bicycling companion. Your veterinarian can evaluate the following aspects of your dog. Check off the boxes as your vet reviews each, and write any notes in the spaces provided.

☐ **CARDIOVASCULAR FITNESS**

_____

_____

_____

_____

☐ **VISION**

_____

_____

_____

_____

☐ **RANGE OF MOTION**

_____

_____

_____

☐ **HIPS AND ELBOWS (TO MAKE SURE THEY'RE NOT DYSPLASTIC)**

_____

_____

_____

Your vet can also advise you on whether the activity you've chosen is suited to your dog. Your dog might be overweight or just not built right for a particular sport. It doesn't have to stop you from getting active together, though. Just because your pug isn't suited to jogging doesn't mean she won't excel in the more leisurely sport of tracking. Basset hounds, bullmastiffs, and many other breeds aren't well suited to agility trials, but they can still compete as long as you take precautions and run them only on courses that don't have so many of the tight twists and turns beloved by some agility judges.

Conditioning Your Dog

All dogs need regular exercise to stay healthy, but canine athletes need conditioning to build up their stamina and improve their athletic performance. The following facts should help you appreciate how much work goes into conditioning a dog:

- ❧ Top herding dogs can cover as much as 100 miles a day.

- ❧ Field trial and hunting dogs must run or walk for miles all day long, as well as retrieve from cold and sometimes rough water.

- ❧ Sled dogs may race 1,200 miles in less than ten days.

Whatever sport you try, walking is the best and easiest way to start conditioning your dog. Depending on his age, size, and general level of health, begin with short walks on leash. Puppies or overweight dogs might start by walking a quarter mile, or whatever distance you can go in five minutes. (Most people can walk a mile in twenty minutes.) Gradually work up to a half mile and then a mile. Keep track of your dog's progress using the following chart:

Date	Type of Activity	Distance	Time

Remember that high-impact exercise such as running or jumping on hard surfaces is detrimental to a young dog's musculo-skeletal development. The growth plates of large-breed dogs don't close until they're fourteen to eighteen months old (small breeds at ten to twelve months of age), so avoid jogging, running, or taking your dog over high jumps until he reaches physical maturity.

Exercise Physiology

Once your dog is at a basic level of fitness, you can start conditioning him for a specific activity. Like any athlete, your dog needs strength, flexibility, and stamina. To help him achieve peak performance, it's important to understand your dog's musculoskeletal system and recognize signs of lameness. By monitoring your dog's response to workouts, you can help prevent the muscle aches and pains that come with too much exercise.

When he's competing, plan to exercise your dog for half an hour every day (with one day off every week for rest). Dogs that compete only seasonally—in field trials, for instance—can stay in shape with a daily fifteen-minute workout, increasing to half an hour daily a couple of months before the season begins. Break up this chunk of time by focusing on different aspects of fitness.

Types of Exercise

Running isn't the only exercise dogs need. Just like humans, dogs can improve skills like strength, balance, and flexibility. Maintaining these skills keeps your dog feeling good and helps prevent injury. Try the following exercises:

- 🐾 **STRENGTH AND STAMINA:** Take him jogging, run him alongside a bicycle, play fetch with a ball or dumbbell, take him swimming, or allow him to run off-leash in a safe, enclosed area. If you're highly motivated and have money to burn, consider investing in a canine treadmill for convenience on rainy, snowy, or hot days.

- 🐾 **BALANCE AND COORDINATION:** Have him "walk the plank"—walk across a fallen tree trunk or a wooden board. This will improve both balance and coordination. Also try laying a ladder on the ground and having your dog step over the rungs.

- 🐾 **FLEXIBILITY:** Teach your dog tricks, such as bows, spins, and waves. Walk him in circles and figure eights. Even if you don't compete in agility, consider setting up some weave poles in your backyard. If weave poles aren't an option, teach your dog to sit up for a treat — a good back-strengthener.

Other types of exercise can help your dog improve balance and develop specific skills. Have him practice stepping on and off objects and stepping over a bar (such as a broomstick) on the ground or a very low jump. Walk him on leash on both level and uneven surfaces so he's accustomed to both. Change pace frequently, moving from a slow walk to a fast walk and back again or from a walk to a trot and back to a walk. If you compete in obedience, make sure to teach your dog to heel on both sides so that he stays supple.

Warm Up and Cool Down

Any time you exercise your dog, warm her up first and cool her down afterward. This is the best way to prevent injuries.

WARM UP

* Get the blood flowing with a short walk or jog. The warm-up stimulates the delivery of increased oxygen and nutrients to the muscles.

* Have your dog do some stretches to limber up the tendons and ligaments. Play bows (front legs outstretched as though she's bowing) are one great stretch, and spins and waves will also loosen her up. Teach your dog to do bends by having her face you and then reach to either side to get a treat. This is great for loosening the neck and body muscles.

* Give a quick all-over massage to loosen stiff muscles and joints.

COOL DOWN

* Cool her down with a slow five-minute walk. This allows the muscles to release the waste products that can cause stiffness.

* Let her drink small amounts of water at a time as she cools down.

* Pay attention to your dog's gait as you walk to make sure she doesn't show any signs of stiffness or lameness.

* End the cool-down period by running your hands over her body to check for any sore areas that may need attention.

Dealing with Injuries

Unfortunately, injuries are bound to happen in any physical activity. There's always the chance that something will go wrong. Dogs can suffer broken bones, tail injuries, anterior cruciate ligament (ACL) tears, and foot pad damage, to name only a few. The following sections describe some of the common problems that can affect different types of athletic dogs, how to recognize them, and what to do for them. However, there are a few preventative measures you can take to be prepared in the case of an injury:

* Supplement your athletic dog with the nutraceuticals chondroitin and glucosamine as a preventive measure. They might not prevent injury, but they may help strengthen cartilage and ensure that injuries are less serious.

* Keep a cold pack and warm compress on hand. Gauze wrap will help you loosely attach the pack or compress to the affected area. Your other option is to spend some quality time with your dog by holding it in place for fifteen minutes, maybe while you're watching television.

🐾 A muzzle is a good item to have around, especially if your dog gets touchy when in pain. Even if he doesn't mean to, your dog might react with a bite when you touch an injured area. The muzzle keeps you both protected in this case.

Musculoskeletal Injuries

Broken bones, knee injuries, and muscle sprains and strains are a fact of life for athletic dogs. A field dog can trip in a hole and break his leg, his back, or his neck. Knee injuries such as cruciate ligament tears can occur in any sport that involves jumping or twisting. Lots of dogs injure toes in any number of activities, particularly agility. Any dog that's not well conditioned or that doesn't get a good warm up before activity is prone to muscle sprains and strains. An athletic dog's musculoskeletal system takes a beating, which is why it's so important to emphasize strength and flexibility.

The following list contains information about some common musculoskeletal injuries:

🐾 **ACL TEARS:** The ACL is the knee's major stabilizing ligament. The wear and tear on limbs from participating in agility or advanced obedience puts dogs at risk for this injury, which occurs when the knee twists suddenly or hyperextends. The result is sudden rear leg lameness and a swollen, painful knee joint. The latest surgical repair for this kind of injury is called a TPLO: tibial plateau leveling osteotomy. Hydrotherapy may be recommended for dogs recovering from ACL surgery.

❧ **BURSITIS OR TENDONITIS:** These are inflammations of a bursa (a small sac between a tendon and a bone) or a tendon (a tough, fibrous band or cord of connective tissue). Both are commonly seen in the biceps tendon, which is shown in dogs as shoulder lameness, and is usually caused by chronic ongoing overactivity. Bursitis and tendonitis are diagnosed by extending the shoulder and putting pressure on the biceps tendon or bursa. If it's painful, your dog will tell you. Therapies that can help include massage, stretching, hot and cold compresses, and therapeutic ultrasound.

❧ **JOINT SPRAINS:** Sprains occur when the ligaments surrounding a joint suddenly stretch or tear. Dogs with sprains have pain and swelling at the joint. They can usually put some weight on the leg but walk with a limp. Rest is the best treatment for a sprain. To help reduce swelling, apply cold packs (a chemical pack wrapped in a towel) three or four times a day for the first twenty-four hours, leaving them on for fifteen to thirty minutes at a time. For the next two or three days, apply warm (not hot), moist compresses to the area, following the same schedule as for cold packs.

Muscle Tears, Strains, and Sprains

When a muscle is stretched beyond its normal length, the result can be a tear, sprain, or strain. This type of injury often occurs after strenuous fieldwork or other activities that involve long periods of running. The injured area is often close to but doesn't involve a joint and is usually painful, hot, and swollen. Once your veterinarian rules out joint disease or a ligament tear as the source of the problem, she will probably recommend at least three weeks of rest, accompanied by cold and heat therapy. Massage or acupuncture may also help.

Broken Bones

A fracture can occur in any sport. All it takes is for a dog to fall off an agility A-frame, step in a hole, or otherwise suffer a bone-breaking trauma. Suspect a broken bone if your dog is unable to put weight on a limb. You'll know for sure she has a broken bone if it's a compound fracture because the bone juts out from the skin.

In the event of a broken bone, splint it the way you found it. Don't try to straighten the limb out; you could make it worse. Keep the dog as still as possible, and get her to the veterinarian.

A dog with a fracture will need surgery to repair the broken bone. Until it heals, the bone will need to be held in position with pins and metal plates or with a splint and cast, depending on where the break occurs. Once the bone has healed, exercise, hydrotherapy, and other therapies can help rebuild muscle strength and flexibility.

Back and Neck Injuries

Tight, twisty agility courses and rigid weave poles are often the cause of back and neck injuries in dogs, as are the twists and turns of a lure course and the spinal compression that occurs every time an advanced obedience or flyball dog lands following a jump. Even if a dog isn't injured during a sport, the underlying arthritis caused by strain on the joints can precipitate problems later from a more trivial action, such as jumping off the sofa.

Rest and pain relief are often the best cures for back and neck injuries. Rest doesn't just mean refraining from a sport; it means close confinement and only brief walks on leash so your dog can relieve himself. The typical rest period is two to four weeks. In addition to analgesics for pain relief, your veterinarian may also prescribe corticosteroids to help reduce swelling and inflammation. A dog with paralysis may need surgery to repair the damage. Stiffness and back pain from arthritis can be treated with rest and nonsteroidal anti-inflammatory pain relievers such as carprofen and etodolac.

Foot Injuries and Toe Trauma

From agility to field trials, herding to sled-dog racing, every canine athlete is prone to foot and toe injuries. Foot pads can become worn down (a common problem in herding dogs). Feet can get cut, and paw pads can become dry and cracked from over-use or exposure to cold. A toe injury might sound trivial, but it can be serious enough to lead to a dog's retirement from a sport. Retrievers and agility dogs are especially prone to toe injuries, which can range from a torn-off toenail to a sprained, dislocated, or broken toe. Dogs can get toe injuries from hitting the toe too hard against something, stepping in a hole, or landing wrong from a jump. Many agility dogs suffer toe injuries from A-frame slats.

Here are some tips for caring for your active dog's feet and toes:

* To treat minor cuts, clean out the wound and bandage the foot. Give it time to heal before your dog returns to his activity.

- Keep dry, cracked paw pads well moisturized, and clean your dog's feet after he's been out in snowy or icy conditions. This helps remove harsh deicing chemicals that may be on sidewalks or roads.

- Have an X ray done if you think your dog has a toe injury. Toes may heal on their own but sometimes require surgery. An X ray may be necessary to spot hairline fractures.

Tail Trouble

A condition that commonly affects hunting dogs goes by a variety of names: cold tail, limber tail syndrome, broken tail, dead tail, and broken wag. They all refer to a condition in which the dog's tail hangs limp from the base or is held horizontal for three or four inches and then drops down. Painful but relatively harmless, cold tail can be associated with swimming, a bath in water that's too cold or too warm, or even after any activity that involves a lot of tail action. The tail usually returns to normal within a few days. To shorten recovery time, ask your veterinarian to prescribe an appropriate anti-inflammatory drug as soon as you notice the condition.

Notes and Observations

Use the following spaces to mark down any observations you've made about your dog's response to physical activity, proneness to injury, recovery time, and any treatments he's received. Also mark down pertinent dates, such as those for specific injuries or medication pre-scriptions. During your next visit to the vet, bring out this list and discuss your concerns, ask questions, and record new information.

_____

_____

_____

_____

_____

_____

_____

_____

_____

_____

_____

_____

_____

_____

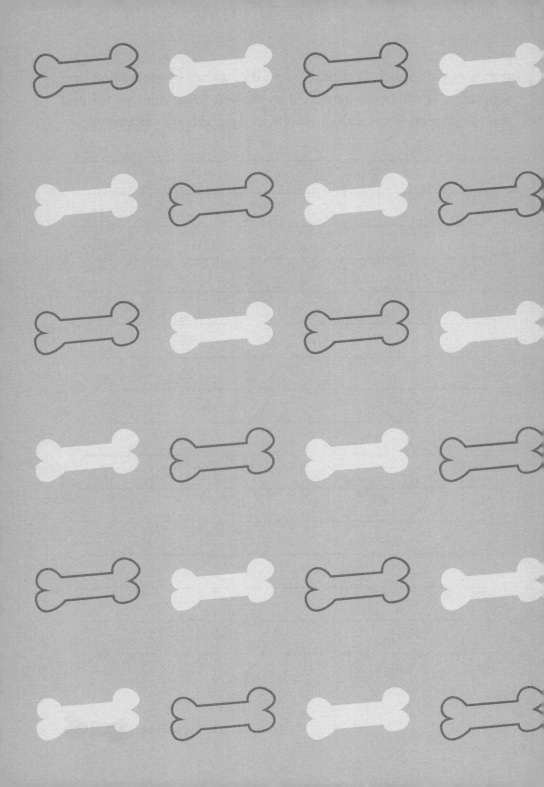

chapter 9

Socializing Your Dog

Exploring the Environment

A big part of socializing your dog is acquainting her with the environment around him. Take your puppy as many places as possible so she becomes a savvy traveler who is accustomed to elevators, stairways, manholes, and grates. Accustom her to walking on a variety of surfaces such as gravel, wire, sand, cobblestone, linoleum, and brick. Because some puppies prefer to eliminate only in their own backyard, teach her to eliminate on command in different areas, so weekend trips and the like won't be a problem.

If you want to foster enjoyment of the water and your puppy isn't a natural pond-puppy, walk her on leash on the shoreline. Once she is at ease with that, venture into the water. Gently tighten the leash as you go, forcing her to swim a couple feet before you let her return to the shore. Never throw a puppy into the water.

Take notes on how she reacts to the following surfaces and stimuli:

🐾 Slick hardwood or tile floors:

_____

_____

🐾 Stairs:

_____

_____

🐾 Falling rain:

_____

_____

🐾 Puddles:

_____

_____

🐾 Falling snow:

_____

_____

☙ Deep snow:

_____

_____

☙ Shallow water:

_____

_____

☙ Deep water:

_____

_____

☙ Thunderstorms:

_____

_____

☙ Piled dry leaves:

_____

_____

☙ Sand (beach):

_____

_____

* Large rocks:

_____

_____

* Gravel or small pebbles:

_____

_____

Meeting People

It's important to socialize your pup to people, making sure he gets plenty of experiences with both genders and a variety of races and ages. Go to the park, a parade, the beach, or the area around a shopping center. Bring some of your dog's favorite kibble or some other tasty treats and have strangers ask him to sit for a greeting and a treat. The reward will teach him to always be polite around those he doesn't know.

Occasionally, leave your puppy in the care of a trustworthy, levelheaded friend for fifteen minutes, an hour, or a day. Your objective is to teach the pup to be self-assured in your absence; therefore, don't say goodbye or hello to the pup. Treat the situation as a nonevent so your pup is less likely to experience separation anxiety. A confident dog allows guests into the house with little fanfare, but he will be alert should something go wrong. He is sure of himself and can be depended upon for a steady temperament. He is not overly aggressive toward strangers or other dogs. A skittish dog—one that lacks confidence—is one that is unsure of people or other dogs. His behavior can be unpredictable.

Also think about items people carry and equipment they use. Expose your pup to the following items and record his reaction:

❧ Wheelchair:

_____

_____

❧ Cane:

_____

_____

❧ Bicycle:

_____

_____

❧ Lawn mower:

_____

_____

❧ Roller skates:

_____

_____

- ❧ Vacuum cleaner:

_____

_____

- ❧ Musical instrument:

_____

_____

- ❧ Umbrella:

_____

_____

Meeting Other Animals

Let your dog get to know other animals—cats, chickens, horses, goats, birds, guinea pigs, lizards, and of course, other puppies and dogs. Often, upon meeting a new species, a puppy is startled, then curious, and then perhaps bold or aggressive. For her own protection and for the protection of the other animal, always keep your pup leashed so you can control her distance and stop unwanted behaviors by enforcing obedience commands. Here are some other tips for introducing your dog to other animals:

☙ Always approach a new animal in a relaxed manner and avoid any situation that would intimidate the average puppy, like a group of excited Great Danes rushing at her.

☙ Be prepared for any of three reactions to a new animal: walking up to check it out and sniff, apprehensive barking, or running away.

☙ No matter her response, remain silent. If she is thinking rationally and investigating her environment, don't draw attention to yourself by talking, praising, or petting. Allow her to explore uninterrupted. She is entertaining herself and being educated at the same time.

☙ If your puppy lacks confidence or displays fear, don't console her—this will reinforce her fear. Use the leash to prevent her from running away. If she is still slightly uncomfortable, drop some tasty bits of food (like slivers of hot dog) on the ground.

☙ When introducing a new puppy to your current dog or cat, remember that your established pet considers your home its territory. If possible, try and introduce the animals on neutral ground—maybe in a friend's yard. It's very important to make sure neither of the animals becomes afraid of the other, or one will quickly become a bully.

Riding in the Car

As soon as your puppy is large enough, teach him to enter and exit the car on command. Practice this by leashing him, walking him up to the car, and commanding him to go in as you give him a boost. Invite him out of the car by calling, "Come," as you gently pull the leash. Practice this several times a day until he goes in and out on command.

Also keep the following in mind to prepare your pup to be a passenger:

- As a first step, decide where you'd like him to ride. Crating is the safest option. If it isn't the most convenient, try a puppy seatbelt, which is available at many pet shops or by mail order.

- Don't feed your puppy prior to riding if he has a tendency toward carsickness.

- It is a good idea to keep the air temperature inside the car comfortably cool, but if you roll down a window, choose one that your puppy cannot stick his head out of. Additionally, you'll reduce the chance of motion sickness by avoiding bumpy roads.

- Leaving a dog in an unattended car in the summer is extremely dangerous. Even if it's cool and cloudy in the morning, the sun could still poke through by mid-afternoon. Even cracking all the windows won't help much, as the temperature in your car could quickly climb above 100 degrees.

Socializing Safely

Perhaps your veterinarian advised you against exposing your puppy while his immune system is developing, but you fear the risks of neglecting to socialize him during this critical period. Though you may not be able to walk him around the big city, you can start a socialization program at home:

- ❧ Desensitize him to noises by letting him play with an empty plastic half-gallon milk jug or big metal spoon.

- ❧ Accustom him to walking on a variety of surfaces, such as bubble wrap, big plastic bags, and chicken wire. Put a treat in the middle so he gets rewarded for his bravery.

- ❧ If his experiences with meeting new people will be limited, you can get creative with costumes. Wear hats, masks, and capes; walk with a cane, limp, skip, and hop.

- ❧ Take him for car rides with permission from your veterinarian.

Dealing with a Fearful Dog

Perhaps you have let the first few months of dog ownership go by without really working on socialization, and now your dog gets frightened in strange environments or with unfamiliar people. Or maybe you have been working to socialize your dog, but the lessons haven't worked as well as you hoped. This could be a result of his breed and/or personality. For example, working and herding breeds are notoriously more suspicious of new people and things. Whatever the reason, don't panic! You can still work on this problem. Sooner is better, but it's never too late to try.

Here are some guidelines for working with your anxious pup:

- ❧ Keep in mind that building confidence in a fearful dog is time-consuming. Don't expect miracles overnight.

- ❧ Be flexible, allow for regression, and be prepared for changes to your plan.

- ❧ Keep all members of the family, dog sitters, and visiting friends in the loop regarding your dog's progress. You don't want someone accidentally undoing weeks of your hard work.

- ❧ Break your goals down into steps in order to see improvement in a relatively short period of time.

Develop a Plan

Having a plan is absolutely critical when working with a fearful dog. For instance, teaching your dog to make a game out of what she is afraid of, through targeting, is a great way to build her confidence. If you practice targeting enough, it will become second nature to your dog, and she will learn to play the game regardless of what else is going on around her.

Maybe your dog is afraid of strange men, for example. You might start off by using a male member of your family whom your dog likes and teaching her to target the person's hand. Once you're ready to move on to trying it with a stranger, remember that it will take time and patience. The task should be broken down into pieces. For example, try the following steps and take notes on the dog's reaction to each:

1. Have the stranger sit in a chair and ignore the dog at first.

_____

_____

_____

2. Next, have the stranger drop small pieces of treats around his feet, and let your dog take her time eating them.

_____

_____

_____

3. If your dog is too scared to eat, break it down into something even easier, like having the person lie on the couch or sit a greater distance away. Your dog's appetite is a good indicator of her comfort level.

_____

_____

_____

4. After the dog relaxes enough to eat the treats, gradually change the variables so that eventually the dog is able to target the person's hand for a treat.

_____

_____

_____

Don't jump right into targeting with strange people. This method will be successful only if you work with your dog extensively, first to teach her to target your hand and then the hands of other people she likes. Once you've built up your dog's confidence around familiar people, targeting can then be used to teach your dog to be brave around new people and other scary things. Taking the time to teach your dog to target will be one of the most important training tools you have to help her get over her fears. It will give your dog something constructive to do instead of being scared.

Be Organized and Consistent

Fearful dogs do not suddenly become confident, even with lots of training. The best approach is having a determined attitude and setting clear, achievable goals. Being consistent and specific about how you want your dog to react and behave is particularly important in the case of an apprehensive dog.

In order to remain consistent in your efforts with your scared pup, you might want to create and maintain a schedule. Get the whole family involved with your plan. Use the following chart to write out a schedule, and then make a copy to post in a visible location.

Day of the Week	Activity	Person Working with Dog	Progress
Sunday			
Monday			
Tuesday			
Wednesday			
Thursday			
Friday			
Saturday			

Take It to the Next Level

If you are unsuccessful with efforts to bring your dog out of her shell at home, you may want to look into some other options. After all, a phobic and anxious dog is probably going to have a difficult time in life. One option to try is enrolling your dog in a well-organized group training class. Be honest with your instructor about what your goals are, and ask if a group class would be an appropriate place to start with a fearful dog such as yours. Also, if you're considering a doggie day-care facility, talk to the staff about your dog's apprehension. There are doggie day cares that take on special cases, and often the staff is very knowledgeable about these problems. They can help make sure your dog learns to overcome her fears and has an enjoyable experience.

Use the following space to write down notes about any training classes or day-care programs you're considering. Reviewing these notes at the end of your research period, perhaps with the help of your veterinarian, will help you make the best decision.

Facility or Program	Notes

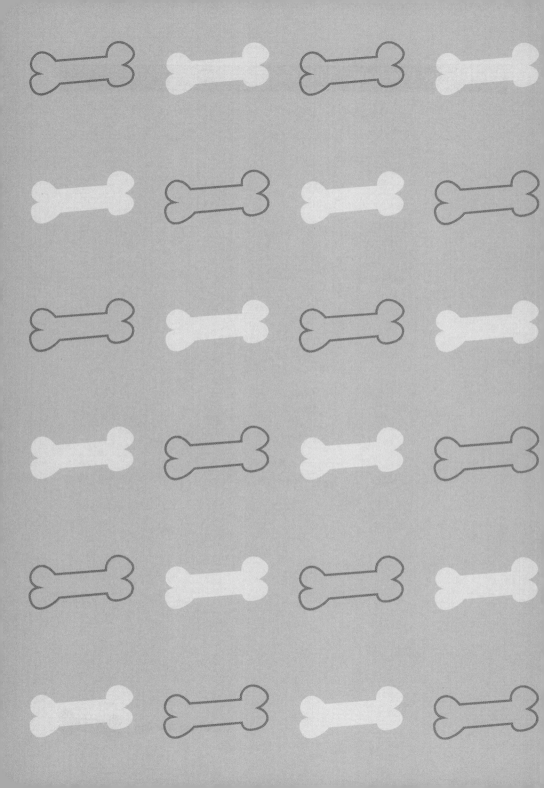

chapter 10

Basic and Obedience Training

Training Basics

Basic behavioral training is essential for any dog. This training isn't designed to teach your dog to do tricks but rather to give you the tools to keep your dog under proper control for his own safety and your peace of mind. Proper basic training will enable you to trust your dog at home alone without wondering what piece of furniture he's destroying.

In order to get the most out of your training, you need to have the proper equipment. The most important pieces of equipment for basic training are a well-fitted collar, a six-foot leather leash, and a fifteen-foot-long line. Additionally, when working toward off-leash control, you'll need a tab (a short nylon rope) and a fifty-foot light line. All are described in some detail following.

Collars

When you begin training, use the collar your puppy wears around the house. It should be well made and properly fitted. If it's not or he doesn't wear a collar, start with a snug fitting, buckle-type collar, flat or rolled. Consider switching to a slip collar, a prong collar, or a head halter if you would like an extra measure of control because of your dog's size or strength. These items should only be used on older puppies and under the guidance of your veterinarian or an experienced trainer.

- **CHAIN SLIP COLLAR:** This type of collar should fit to be only ½ to 2 inches larger than the thickest part of your puppy's skull. Although collars this small can be difficult to slide on and off, snug collars deliver timelier corrections. This type also stays in place better when properly positioned—high on the neck, just behind the ears, with the rings just under the puppy's right ear. So that the slip collar will loosen after corrections, it's important to put this collar on correctly. You'll know if you've got the collar on correctly if the links slide easily when tightened or loosened.

- **NYLON SLIP COLLAR:** Neither round nor flat nylon slip collars offer the slide and release action of a chain, but they do deliver stronger corrections than buckle collars. As with any collar, the nylon slip should only be tightened momentarily while correcting; constant tension means the puppy isn't being told when he's doing well and when he's doing poorly.

- **PRONG COLLAR:** Strong or easily distracted puppies may benefit by use of a prong or pinch collar. The prongs come in four sizes: micro, small, medium, and large. The length is adjustable by removing or adding prongs. Some people think prong

 The Everything Dog Owner's Organizer

collars look like instruments of torture, but they're actually a very humane tool when properly used. If you want to use one, have an experienced trainer show you how to properly fit and work with it.

Leashes

To teach commands and mannerly walking, and to "umbilical cord" your puppy (lead him with his leash tied to your belt), use a six-foot leather leash. The proper width of the leash depends on your pup's weight. See the following table for guidelines.

Weight of puppy	Width of leash
15 pounds	$^{1}/_{4}$ inch
16 to 45 pounds	$^{1}/_{2}$ inch
46 to 75 pounds	$^{3}/_{4}$ inch
76 pounds and up	1 inch

To train your puppy to accept the leash, start by putting on his buckle-type collar and lightweight leash. For ten to thirty minutes, three times a day for a week, watch him drag it around the house or yard. Better still, attach the lead prior to playtime with another puppy or a favorite toy. He'll step on it, scratch his neck, refuse to move, or maybe even scream, all of which you should ignore. Since many puppies like to chew the lead, you may need to thoroughly coat it before each session with a chewing deterrent like Bitter Apple spray.

When he is comfortable about dragging the leash, pick up the handle and coax him to walk on your left side by carrying and squeezing an interesting squeaky toy. If he really fights you, attach the leash handle to a doorknob and let him struggle with that while you drink a cup of coffee. Watch him out of the corner of your eye to confirm that his antics aren't endangering him. Repeat the procedure for five or ten minutes at a time until he is relaxed before attempting to walk with the leash in hand again.

long line

Many exercises are done on a fifteen-foot nylon cord called a long line. Since many pet stores don't carry them, just go to a hardware store and buy a swivel snap and fifteen feet of nylon cord—a quarter-inch in diameter for a medium-sized puppy and an eighth of an inch smaller or larger for small and large puppies, respectively. Tie the snap on one end and make a loop for your thumb on the other.

light line and glove

The light line is a fifty-foot nylon cord. Use parachute cord for large puppies, Venetian blind cord for medium or small puppies, and nylon twine for tiny breeds. The light line is tied to the tab and used as you make the transition to off-lead work. When you're working with the tab and light line, wear a form-fitted gardening glove to ensure a better grip and to prevent rope burn.

retractable leashes

These popular leads come in lengths from eight to thirty-two feet. You can let the puppy venture away and explore without getting his legs entangled, thanks to a constant, slight amount of tension. Be aware, however, that these leashes can teach your dog to pull, as there is always tension. Never let your dog get around a corner when using these leashes.

The buttons on the easy-to-grip plastic handle allow you to lock it at a length as short as four inches for some models, or as long as the total length or any length in between.

To make your puppy adapt to your pace and stay by your side using a retractable leash, lock it in the shortest position. The plastic handle allows you to give a stronger tug than the leash allows, which is especially useful if space is limited or footing is bad. When you arrive at his potty area or meet up with a canine playmate, unlock the lead and, with your permission, let the puppy pull out the length.

Leash Walking

Begin the next phase of your training once your puppy is content to be near you no matter what distractions are around. This step teaches him to walk on a loose leash at your left side. Attach the six-foot leash to his collar and put your right thumb in the handle. Enclose your fingers around the straps of the handle below. Hold the midsection of the leash with the right hand, too, so your left hand is free. The leash should have just enough slack to touch the middle of your left thigh when your right hand is at your hip. Use the following points as a guide:

- **IF YOUR PUPPY CONSISTENTLY PULLS:** When your puppy forges ahead, open and close your hand to release the slack, then grip the handle as you pivot and run away. Do this when his shoulder is only inches ahead of your leg, rather than waiting until he is tugging at the end of the leash or lunging frantically ahead. When your puppy is running after you, pick up the slack in the leash again and stop dead.

- **IF YOUR PUPPY RUNS RIGHT PAST YOU:** Pivot once again and sneak away before he bolts ahead. If your puppy is a charger, watch his body language closely so it becomes easy to anticipate when to do multiple direction changes.

- **IF YOUR PUPPY ATTEMPTS TO LAG:** Reduce the slack by tightening the leash a bit—about one to five inches—as you briskly walk forward. The puppy may bump into the back of your legs for the next few steps but that, along with the fact that the leash tightens against your left thigh with every step, will encourage him to return to your left side. Remember to keep your left hand off the leash so nothing interferes with your thigh pulling into the leash.

The Everything Dog Owner's Organizer

Getting Started

These twelve steps will guide you as you begin to train your dog:

1. Decide what you'd like your puppy to do.
2. Decide what clear visual or auditory signal you will use to initiate the desired action.
3. Give verbal commands using the right tonality, inflection, and volume (don't plead, mumble, or shout).
4. Preface verbal commands with the puppy's name. The name and command should sound like one word ("Buster heel," rather than "Buster . . . heel.") Just one exception: Don't use his name in conjunction with the "Stay" command, since hearing his name infers that he should be attentive and ready to go.
5. Say the command only once.
6. Make an association. While teaching, give the command as you make the puppy do the action (for example, say, "Sit" as you pull up on the collar and push down on the pup's rear).
7. Give commands only when you can enforce them; otherwise, you risk teaching disobedience.
8. Decide on reinforcement. How are you going to show the puppy what to do? Unlike the other eleven steps, this will change depending on your puppy's stage in training.
9. Show your appreciation with precisely timed praise.
10. End every command with a release word, such as "Okay!"
11. Test your puppy's understanding by working him around distractions before progressing to the next level.

12. Don't take obedience for granted—puppies forget, get lazy, become distracted, and inevitably fail to respond to familiar commands. Especially if he rarely makes a mistake, correct him so he understands the rules haven't changed.

Clicker and Treat Training

Clickers are often used for training service dogs and for teaching tricks. Simply put, when the puppy does something desirable, she is given a signal (usually a distinct sound) that the behavior is right, offered a food reward and, eventually, taught to do it on command possibly without the food. Many trainers use the click of a tin cricket to signify the appropriateness of a behavior. For instance, if the objective is to teach a puppy to sneeze, the trainer would wait for her to do so, click the tin cricket, and offer a treat or other reward. Because of the power of association, soon the puppy will react to the sound of the clicker with as much delight as the treat. Therefore, if the puppy is working far away or retrieving and can't be given a treat, the clicker communicates that she is doing a great job. Of course, many people do the same thing with the word "Good!" instead of the clicker.

Using food to train is another option. There are basically three ways to use food:

* As a lure to get the puppy to perform a task

* As a reward for completing an already learned task

* As reinforcement for behaviors offered by the puppy (as in click-and-treat training)

Most people use treats and body language as a lure because it is the fastest way to entice the puppy to perform a task. But beware: There is a huge gap between following a lure and obeying a command. To bridge that gap, learn how to enforce your commands with your hands and leash. This will also prove invaluable if your puppy isn't interested in the treat because she's full or distracted.

Obedience Training

While basic training will teach a puppy how to behave properly in general, obedience training will give you the ability to get your dog to do what you want, when you want him to. Not only that, but obedience training is the foundation to more advanced tricks. These are the basic obedience skills:

* Sit

* Stay

* Down

* Heel

* Come

* Wait

Sit

Teach the "Sit" command by putting your puppy on your left side, holding his collar with your right hand, and putting your left hand on his loin just in front of his hip bones and behind his rib cage. Command "Sit" as you pull upward on his collar and push downward on his loin. Talk, pet, and praise, but don't let the puppy move. When necessary, reposition him by pushing him back into the sit as you tighten up on the collar. After a few seconds, release with "Okay!" If he is rigid and won't budge, move him forward and walk him into the sit.

record your progress

Use the following space to record your dog's progress with learning the "Sit" command.

_____

_____

_____

_____

_____

_____

_____

_____

The Everything Dog Owner's Organizer

_____

_____

_____

_____

_____

_____

_____

_____

_____

Stay

While your dog is sitting, hold the leash taut over his head. Say, "Stay" in a firm voice, and then take one step back from him. While looking at your puppy, count silently to three, then release with "Okay!" and praise your puppy. Do this once more, and if your puppy stays for the whole count of three, give him a big hug and do something else for a while. If your puppy moves his head or wags his tail, that's acceptable, but you should correct scooting forward, rotating, and attempts to stand by pulling up on the leash and repeat.

If your puppy tries to lie down, tighten the leash enough to prevent him from lowering comfortably into the down position and give him praise as he realizes he doesn't have enough slack to lie down. Loosen the lead and prepare to repeat this sequence many times during the next week of training if your puppy is one who is inclined to recline.

You may be wondering why you should care about lying down on the sit stay if you're not thinking of doing any competitive obedience. The answer is simple. You need your puppy to sit, not lie down, so you can look in his mouth, administer medication or ear ointment, or wipe dirt off his paws. Say what you mean and mean what you say to avoid confusion in all areas of training.

record your progress

Use the following space to record your dog's progress with learning the "Stay" command.

_____

_____

_____

_____

_____

_____

_____

_____

_____

_____

_____

_____

_____

_____

Down

With your puppy in the sit position and a tasty treat in your hand, hold the treat near his nose so he gets interested in it. Without letting him eat it but so that his nose follows your hand, start to slowly lower your hand toward the floor and toward you. The idea is to get his front end to come down toward your hand and then follow your hand out until he's lying down.

Many puppies stand up while they follow the lure with their nose. You can either keep a hand on his hindquarters to keep them down, or you can sneak the food lure under a chair so that he has to scooch on his tummy to follow it. As soon as he's down, feed the treat and say, "Good down!" Then release with "Okay!"

Once your puppy knows what "Down" means, practice rapid-fire downs by commanding "Down," giving praise and releasing with "Okay" and repeating the sequence for one minute, three times per training session. Exceptional puppies may learn the verbal "Down" command in a week. With an average of twenty repetitions per day, most puppies will down 50 percent of the time after one month.

record your progress

Use the following space to record your dog's progress with learning the "Down" command.

_____

_____

_____

_____

_____

_____

_____

_____

_____

_____

Heel

The "Heel" command teaches the puppy to walk on your left side—regardless of your pace or direction—and to sit when you stop. As the puppy learns to heel and you learn how to teach him to move precisely, a deeper learning takes place for both of you. To remain in position, the puppy's awareness, watchfulness, and willingness grow.

Your goal is to teach your puppy to maintain heel position, on your left side, with his shoulder aligned with yours, and his body three inches from your leg. The position is the same whether you're moving forward, turning, or standing still. When you stop, your puppy should sit automatically.

To begin, hold the leash in your right hand with your right thumb through the loop and four fingers holding the slack. Say, "Buster, heel" as you begin walking. Prepare to stop by grabbing the collar with your right hand and using your left to place his rear end into a sitting position so his right front foot is alongside your left ankle.

As you walk along preparing to halt, control your puppy's position using the fold-over maneuver. Grab the leash with your left hand and hold it taut over puppy's head, then use your right to grip the braiding or stitching of the leash just above the snap. Next, take your left hand off the leash and use it to place puppy in a sit in perfect heel position as you halt.

If your puppy forges ahead, drop the slack of the leash, grip the handle, hold your hands at your waistline, and run away. As the puppy returns to your side, return to the original leash grip, holding the slack, as you continue walking.

If your puppy lags behind, say, "Good puppy!" as you spring ahead by taking a puddle jump with your left leg first. As you do this, your left thigh will pull the leash, and your puppy, back to the heel position. The jump ahead will also prevent the puppy from crossing behind you to the right side.

going from heel to sit

Before you begin this, your puppy should reliably sit 80 percent of the time when you ask him. He shouldn't need to be touched or retold. What you want him to do is stop heeling and go into the sit position. Here's what to do.

1. Say, "Buster, heel," and move off on your left foot.
2. Prepare to stop by gathering the leash in both hands.
3. As you finish your last step, pull up on the leash, and say, "Sit." You'll need to practice this over and over. Don't wear

yourself or your puppy out. If he doesn't get it the first time, try once more and, if you're successful, end on a positive note. If he doesn't get it the second time, go on to something else and start again later.

learning to heel with turns

You'll need to practice turning while you're heeling. This helps stop tendencies to heel too far from or too close to you and to correct slight forging and sniffing of the ground. You want to practice turning sharply.

Use the "Jackie Gleason left turn" to stop slight forging, crowding, and sniffing of the ground: Turn ninety degrees to the left, then step perpendicularly into your puppy so your left foot and leg slide or step behind his front legs. Shuffle into him until he becomes attentive and moves back to the left side. Practice slowing your pace abruptly, then turn left immediately if your puppy's shoulder is even one inch ahead of yours. If your puppy attempts to cross in front of you to the right side, tighten the leash with your left hand as you continue to step into him.

To stop wideness, sniffing, or lagging, use puddle jump following a right turn. Pivot ninety degrees to your right on your left foot, take a large step in your new direction with the right foot and leap forward with your left leg as if you were jumping over a puddle. As you jump the puddle you should feel the leash against your left thigh, pulling the puppy forward. Steady your leash by holding your right hand against your right hip as you leap.

Jump and praise simultaneously to motivate your puppy. Hold the leash in your right hand so the slack will remain in front of your thighs as you jump.

record your progress

Use the following space to record your dog's progress with learning the "Heel" command.

_____

_____

_____

_____

_____

_____

_____

_____

_____

_____

_____

Come

You want your puppy to learn that when he comes to you when you call him, he will be made to feel like the world's best dog. Coming to you should always be a positive experience. Reward your pup with exuberant praise, tasty treats, a game of fetch, or more time on your walk—whatever it takes to let him know that he did the right thing.

To start, leash your puppy and take him for a walk. If he begins sniffing something, gazing around, or meandering off, call "Buster, come!" Immediately back up quickly as you reel the leash, praising enthusiastically. Kneel down when puppy arrives, heaping him with verbal praise and occasionally slipping him a super-tasty treat. Release with "Okay!" and continue practicing the sequence.

Some puppies will come toward you but stay out of reach or dart right past you. Some owners, without realizing it, encourage the puppy to cut his approach and stay further away by attempting to cradle, caress, or hug the puppy. Petting the puppy as he arrives can create or worsen these recall problems because extending your arms makes it appear you are protecting the space in front of you. Instead, use verbal praise to acknowledge, encourage, and congratulate the puppy's arrival and keep your hands to yourself until he's right with you.

After practicing your reeling recalls twenty or so times, your puppy is probably running toward you faster than you can reel. Now see if he'll leave distractions when you stand still and call, "Come." If he doesn't respond promptly, use a sharp, fast, horizontal jerk toward you as you praise and back up. If he does respond to your command, praise and continue to back up, praising as he nears you.

The goal you want to reach next is to teach your puppy to stop and come when called even if he's running away or you're following him. Here's what to do. Three times this week, create a situation that will cause your puppy to forget his training and pull toward a distraction. For example, ask a fellow puppy owner to go with you on a walk. Instruct him to walk his puppy about ten feet ahead of you. Your puppy is likely to want to catch up to them. As you are walking directly behind your puppy, ask him to come. If he responds, what a good boy! Praise and crouch down to reward him, then release with "Okay!" If he doesn't respond, tug on his leash, back up, call him again, and praise when he turns toward you. Then reel him in.

If your puppy stops when you call him but he doesn't come to you, stay put. Don't chase after him. Pull the leash to let him know you want him to come toward you, then ask again. He should do what you want.

record your progress

Use the following space to record your dog's progress with learning the "Come" command.

_____

_____

_____

_____

_____

_____

_____

_____

_____

_____

_____

_____

Wait

A request that comes in very handy around the house is "Wait." Use this to ask your puppy to wait at the door, go in or out of the door, or when you're out of sight.

The "Stay" command means freeze in the sit, down, or stand position and, therefore, is very restrictive. The "Wait" command, though, allows your puppy to move about, but only within certain areas. You can use it to keep your puppy in the car or out of the kitchen. The only thing "Wait" has in common with "Stay" is that both last until the next direction is given, twenty seconds or twenty minutes later.

Teach the "Wait" command at doorways first. Choose a lightweight door and estimate how wide your puppy's front end is. Open the door two inches more than that as you command "Wait." Stand there with your hand on the knob of the partially open door, ready to bump the puppy's nose with it should he attempt to pass through the opening. Be sure never to shut the door while correcting. Instead, leave the door open with your hand on the door handle, ready to stop attempted departures with an abrupt and silent bump of the door. If necessary, butt him with a quick movement that makes it appear the door is snapping at him every time he tries to peer or charge out. Leash your puppy so if your attempts to deter him fail and he successfully skips across the border, you can step on the leash and prevent his escape.

Practice at familiar and unfamiliar doors as a helper tries to coerce your puppy to leave. Your helper can talk to the puppy and drop food, but your helper shouldn't call your puppy. As your helper remains on the opposite side of the door, engage in lively

Date	Commands Worked On	Number of Repetitions	Notes

Date	Commands Worked On	Number of Repetitions	Notes

The Everything Dog Owner's Organizer

Date	Commands Worked On	Number of Repetitions	Notes

conversation to teach your puppy that even when you are preoccupied, the "Wait" command is enforced. When that lesson has been learned, you'll no longer need the leash.

record your progress

Use the following space to record your dog's progress with learning the "Wait" command.

_____

_____

_____

_____

_____

_____

_____

_____

The Learning Process

Everyone's idea of what constitutes a trained puppy varies. If your definition includes having the ability to control your puppy around distractions and teach her to sit, stay, down, heel, come, and wait,

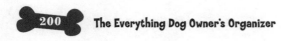

the answer depends on how quickly you can learn basic puppy training skills. If you are willing to devote twenty or twenty-five minutes of daily practice for ten weeks, both you and your puppy are likely to achieve excellent results. Plan your training agenda being sure to note the number of repetitions and specific ways to practice each exercise. Some days it may seem as if you're getting nowhere, but the cumulative effect of this strategy never fails to develop a proficient team.

Use the following charts to keep track of your dog's obedience training progress with each individual command. If you've followed the lessons in this chapter, the obedience skills will include sit, stay, down, heel, come, and wait. The chart has places for the date, commands you worked on, number of repetitions, and any notes you'd like to make about the session. These notes might include how long it took for your dog to show improvement, which skills he seemed to enjoy the most, and which family members have had the most success. Make copies of the blank charts and post them in a visible location. This will make it easy for each family member to document their training sessions and pick up where the last person left off.

All Dogs Are Different

Just like people, all puppies should be evaluated based on their individual temperaments and characteristics. No breed has a patent on problems or virtues. Therefore, stereotyping breeds does more harm than good. You should heed warnings to be extra conscientious because of certain breed tendencies—teaching a sporting puppy to listen to you even in heavily scented fields rather than following his nose; being on the lookout for aggressive tendencies toward other puppies in terrier breeds; or socializing herding breeds a lot, especially when they are four to six months old, so they don't become skittish.

Be Patient

Puppy training is an adventure of sorts: never predictable, sometimes elating, and sometimes tedious. Be optimistic about your puppy's potential but expect her progress to occasionally be slow or nonexistent. Don't, however, abandon your original goals and settle for meager results. Shoddy, half-learned obedience can cause annoying problems or allow them to fester. Many owners give up on training but later decide to give it another try—this time approaching it with far greater determination and achieving far better results. Whether this is your first time around or your last-ditch effort, recognize that a degree of frustration is part of the learning process. If frustration or doubt strikes, keep training. You may be five seconds from a learning breakthrough.

Use Praise As a Training Tool

With some puppies, a word of praise goes a long way. Others appear unaffected by it. Gracious puppy trainers use lots of praise at the right time in the right way to acknowledge and congratulate specific actions, concentration, and worthy intent. Experiment with a variety of ploys to find what delights your puppy no matter what her mood. Whatever you use, your puppy's reaction is the most important indicator that you are on track. Does your type of praise make her eyes bright and get that tail wagging? If she is bored by your technique, working to find out what she likes will improve every part of your relationship.

Use the following space to record different praise techniques you try, as well as your dog's reaction to them. Review these notes the next time you want to use praise as a training tool, and remember what works and what doesn't.

Praise Technique	Your Dog's Reaction

Never praise your puppy if she does her work in a distracted or preoccupied manner; she may think you are praising her inattention. On the flip side, punishment will do little in terms of training a puppy, unless you want to train your puppy to be timid. Generally, a dog will not link punishment to doing something wrong. Regular punishment will only make your puppy afraid of your training sessions.

Remember that your puppy has now learned these commands at home, but she will need to learn to obey in different places, too. Take your dog to a different place at least once a week and practice her commands. Take her to a park or have her accompany you while you're running errands to the bank or the dry cleaner.

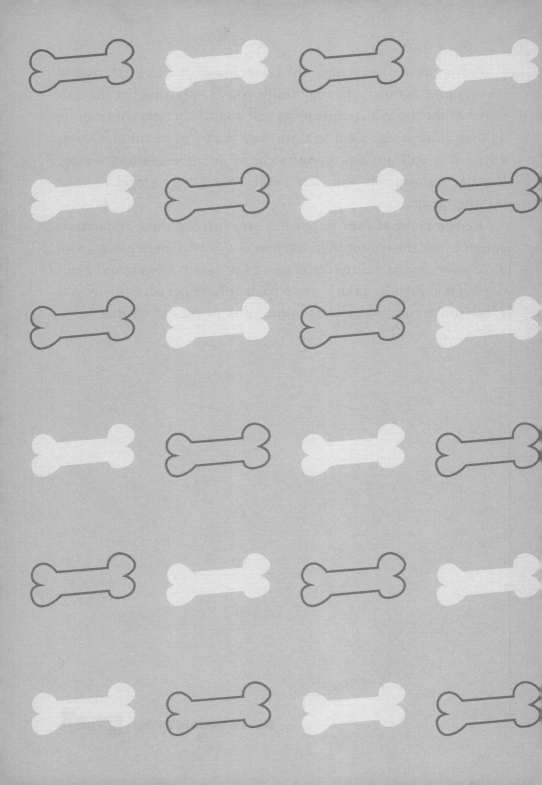

PART 4

Uniquely Yours

About Your Dog

Contact Information

part four
Uniquely Yours

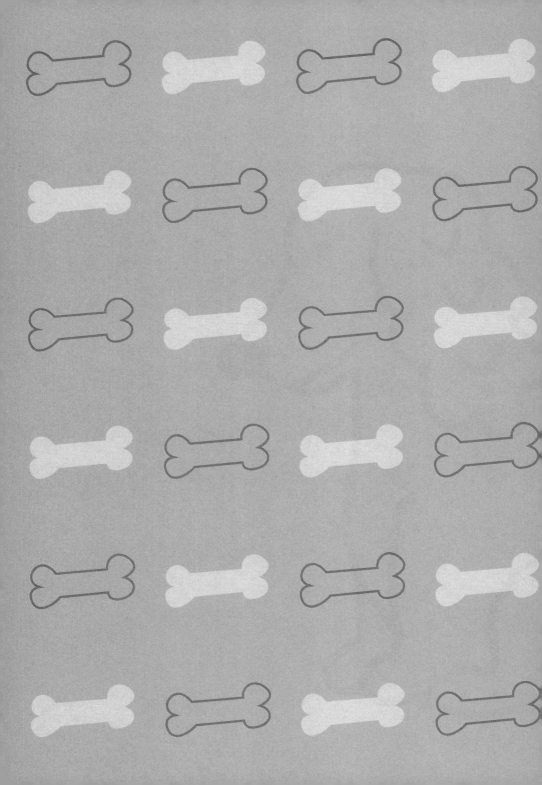

chapter 11

About Your Dog

Keep a Record

It's a good idea to keep a record of all your dog's basic information. This list can be used as a reference during visits to the vet or the groomer, and it can also be a helpful tool to use if your dog ever gets lost. Complete the blanks next to each topic, and remember to include dates for important medical points, like vaccinations and surgeries. Always keep this list up to date and accessible.

IDENTITY AND APPEARANCE

Name

_____

Nickname(s)

_____

Sex

_____

Spayed or neutered?

_____

Date of birth

_____

Date of adoption or purchase

_____

Microchip number

_____

License number

_____

Breed

_____

Coat type

_____

Coat color

_____

Eye color

_____

Ear type

_____

Tail type

_____

Unusual markings

_____

Other

_____

Other

_____

Other

_____

TEMPERAMENT AND PERSONALITY

Personality traits

_____

_____

_____

Good habits

_____

_____

_____

Bad habits

_____

_____

_____

Behavior with strangers

_____

_____

_____

Behavior with children

_____

_____

_____

Behavior with other animals

_____

_____

_____

Athletic ability

_____

_____

_____

HEALTH

Injuries

_____

_____

_____

Illnesses

_____

_____

_____

Medications

_____

_____

_____

Vaccinations

_____

_____

_____

Spay or neuter surgery

_____

_____

_____

Other surgeries

_____

_____

_____

Other

_____

_____

_____

Other

_____

_____

_____

LIKES AND DISLIKES

Likes

_____

_____

Likes

_____

_____

Likes

_____

_____

Likes

_____

_____

Likes

_____

_____

Dislikes

_____

_____

Dislikes

_____

_____

Dislikes

_____

_____

Dislikes

_____

_____

Dislikes

_____

_____

FUN AND FAVORITES

Favorite treats

_____

_____

Favorite toy(s)

_____

_____

Favorite game(s)

_____

_____

Jobs (for instance, fetches the newspaper, brings slippers)

_____

_____

Mastered obedience commands

_____

_____

Favorite tricks

_____

_____

Preferred sleeping spot

_____

_____

Other

_____

_____

Other

_____

_____

Other

_____

_____

Other

_____

_____

Other

_____

_____

Photos

It's a good idea to keep a photo record of your dog's appearance as well as to write down all the details of her appearance and identity. Place and secure photos in the following designated areas. In addition to being a great tool to use if your dog ever gets lost, this section will serve as a fun photo album to flip through with friends and family.

Head from front

Head from side

 222

Body from side

Body from side

The Everything Dog Owner's Organizer

Body from rear

Your dog's arrival

 226   The Everything Dog Owner's Organizer

First birthday

Second birthday

Third birthday

Fourth birthday

 230 The Everything Dog Owner's Organizer

Fifth birthday

Sixth birthday

Seventh birthday

Eighth birthday

 234   The Everything Dog Owner's Organizer

Ninth birthday

Tenth birthday

Eleventh birthday

Twelfth birthday

The Everything Dog Owner's Organizer

Thirteenth birthday

Fourteenth birthday

240 The Everything Dog Owner's Organizer

Fifteenth birthday

Sixteenth birthday

chapter 12

Contact Information

The following is an alphabetized directory of all the important people, facilities, and organizations in your dog's life. Fill in the blank spaces and use this as a reference whenever you need to contact someone on your dog's behalf. Once you've filled in the information, you might even want to make a copy of this list and post it in a visible place in your home, such as on the refrigerator.

ANIMAL CONTROL: _____

Address: _____

Phone number: _____

Directions: _____

_____

_____

BOARDING FACILITY: _____

Address: _____

Phone number: _____

Directions: _____

_____

_____

BREEDER: _____

Address: _____

Phone number: _____

Directions: _____

_____

_____

EMERGENCY CLINIC: _____

Address: _____

Phone number: _____

Directions: _____

_____

_____

EMERGENCY CONTACT: _____

Address: _____

Phone number: _____

Directions: _____

_____

_____

GROOMER: _____

Address: _____

Phone number: _____

Directions: _____

_____

_____

LOCAL DOG CLUB: _____

Address: _____

Phone number: _____

Directions: _____

_____

_____

PET SiTTER: _____

Address: _____

Phone number: _____

Directions: _____

_____

_____

PET SUPPLY STORE: _____

Address: _____

Phone number: _____

Directions: _____

_____

_____

POiSON CONTROL HOTLiNE: _____

Phone number: _____

_____

TRAINER: _____
Address: _____

Phone number: _____

Directions: _____

_____

_____

VETERINARIAN: _____
Address: _____

Phone number: _____

Directions: _____

_____

_____

OTHER: _____
Address: _____

Phone number: _____

Directions: _____

_____

_____

OTHER: _____

Address: _____

Phone number: _____

Directions: _____

_____

_____

OTHER: _____

Address: _____

Phone number: _____

Directions: _____

_____

_____

OTHER: _____

Address: _____

Phone number: _____

Directions: _____

_____

_____

appendix a
Journal Pages

Most dog owners agree that a dog is not just a pet; a dog is a friend, a companion, and a member of the family. So don't be surprised if you come to care about your dog as much as you care about some of the people in your life. After all, what's not to love about a furry little pal who's always happy to see you?

You've already recorded a lot of information in the various sections of this organizer, but these journal pages offer you an opportunity to write down any thoughts, observations, questions, and ideas you have relating to your dog. Some entries might be simple summaries of what you did with your dog that day, while others might be more reflective.

As with any journal, it's helpful to write down the dates of your entries. In the future you'll be able to look back and treasure all the great times you spent with your canine companion.

Date: _____

_____

_____

_____

_____

_____

_____

_____

_____

_____

_____

_____

Date: _____

_____

_____

_____

_____

_____

_____

_____

_____

_____

_____

_____

Date: _____

_____

_____

_____

_____

_____

_____

_____

_____

_____

_____

_____

_____

_____

Date: _____

_____

_____

_____

_____

_____

_____

_____

_____

_____

_____

_____

_____

_____

Date: _____

_____

_____

_____

_____

_____

_____

_____

_____

_____

_____

_____

Date: _____

_____

_____

_____

_____

_____

_____

_____

_____

_____

_____

_____

Date: _____

_____

_____

_____

_____

_____

_____

_____

_____

_____

_____

_____

_____

Date: _____

_____

_____

_____

_____

_____

_____

_____

_____

_____

_____

_____

_____

Date: _____

_____
_____
_____
_____
_____
_____
_____
_____
_____
_____
_____
_____
_____

Date: _____

_____
_____
_____
_____
_____
_____
_____
_____
_____
_____
_____
_____
_____

Date: _____

_____
_____
_____
_____
_____
_____
_____
_____
_____
_____
_____
_____
_____

Date: _____

_____
_____
_____
_____
_____
_____
_____
_____
_____
_____
_____
_____
_____

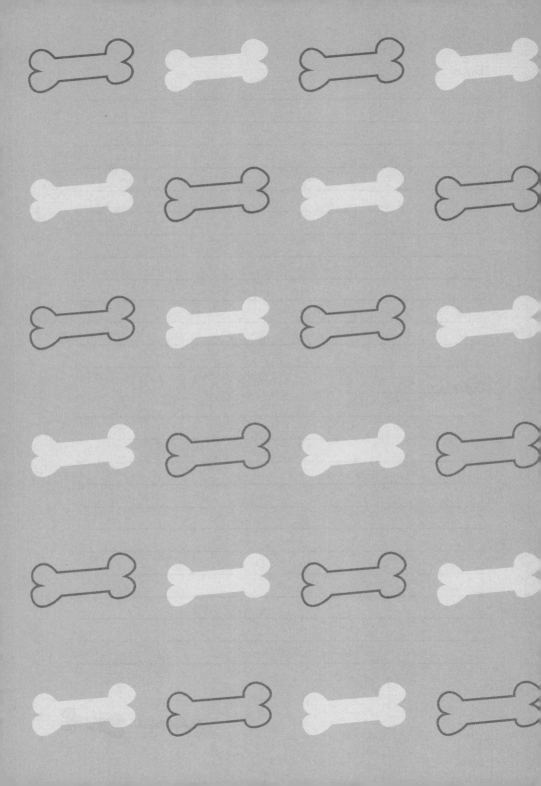

appendix b

Resources

By this point you've absorbed and documented a lot of information! Your pup is on his way to becoming a well behaved, nicely groomed, and very happy part of the family. But there may be topics you'd like to learn more about, such as breed competitions or volunteering with your dog. This appendix is filled with great resources to help you take the next step. From a list of breed registries to lists of helpful Web sites and books, you'll find numerous sources of ideas and information here.

Breed Registries

AMERiCAN KENNEL CLUB
260 Madison Avenue

New York, NY 10016

🖱 www.akc.org

AMERiCAN MiXED BREED OBEDiENCE REGiSTRATiON
179 Niblick Road #113

Paso Robles, CA 93446

🖱 www.amborusa.org

AMERiCAN RARE BREED ASSOCiATiON
9921 Frank Tippett Road

Cheltenham, MD 20623

🖱 www.arba.org

MiXED BREED DOG CLUBS OF AMERiCA
13884 State Route 104

Lucasville, OH 45648

🖱 www.mbdca.tripod.com

UNITED KENNEL CLUB
100 East Kilgore Road

Kalamazoo, MI 49002

🖱 www.ukcdogs.com

Web Sites

Activities

CANINE FREESTYLE FEDERATION
🖱 www.canine-freestyle.org

CANINE PERFORMANCE EVENTS (AGILITY)
🖱 www.k9cpe.com

NASAR SEARCH AND RESCUE DOGS
🖱 www.nasar.org

NATIONAL URBAN SEARCH AND RESCUE RESPONSE SYSTEM
🖱 www.fema.gov/usr/usr__canines.shtm

NORTH AMERICAN DOG AGILITY COUNCIL
🖱 www.nadac.com

NORTH AMERICAN FLYBALL ASSOCIATION

🖱 www.flyball.org

UNITED STATES DOG AGILITY ASSOCIATION

🖱 www.usdaa.com

WORLD CANINE FREESTYLE ORGANIZATION

🖱 www.worldcaninefreestyle.org

Health

AMERICAN ANIMAL HOSPITAL ASSOCIATION

🖱 www.aahanet.org

AMERICAN VETERINARY MEDICAL ASSOCIATION

🖱 www.avma.org

FDA CENTER FOR VETERINARY MEDICINE

🖱 www.fda.gov/cvm

ASPCA ANIMAL POISON CONTROL CENTER

🖱 www.napcc.aspca.org

PURINA PET CARE CENTER
🖱 www.purina.com

Training and Behavior

AMERICAN DOG TRAINER'S NETWORK
🖱 www.thedogsite.org

ASSOCIATION OF PET DOG TRAINERS
🖱 www.apdt.com

CAMPBELL'S PET BEHAVIOR RESOURCES
🖱 www.webtrail.com/petbehavior/index.html

DOG OBEDIENCE AND TRAINING PAGE
🖱 www.dogpatch.org

NATIONAL ASSOCIATION OF DOG OBEDIENCE INSTRUCTORS (NADOI)
🖱 www.nadoi.org

Books

Puppies

101 Essential Tips: Puppy Care, by Bruce Fogle (Dorling Kindersley)

How to Raise a Puppy You Can Live With, by Clarice Rutherford and David H. Neil (Alpine Publications)

I Just Got a Puppy: What Do I Do? by Mordecai Siegal and Matthew Margolis (Fireside)

Puppy Care and Training: A Guide to a Happy, Healthy Pet, by Bardi McLennan (Howell Book House)

The Art of Raising a Puppy, by the Monks of New Skete (Little, Brown)

The Everything® Puppy Book, by Carlo DeVito and Amy Ammen (Adams Media)

The Perfect Puppy: How to Raise a Well-behaved Dog, by Gwen Bailey (Reader's Digest)

Dogs

Selecting the Best Dog for You, by Chris Nelson (TFH)

The Complete Dog Book, by the American Kennel Club (Howell Book House)

The Complete Dog Book for Kids, by the American Kennel Club (Howell Book House)

The Everything® Dog Book, by Carlo DeVito and Amy Ammen (Adams Media)

The Intelligence of Dogs, by Stanley Coren (Free Press)

The Lost History of the Canine Race, by Mary Elizabeth Thurston (Avon)

Health

Dog Doctor, by Mark Evans (Howell Book House)

Dog Owner's Home Veterinary Handbook, by James M. Giffin, M.D., and Liisa D. Carlson, D.V.M. (Howell Book House)

The Consumer's Guide to Dog Food, by Liz Palika (Howell Book House)

The Everything® Dog Health Book, by Kim Campbell Thornton and Debra Eldredge, D.V.M. (Adams Media)

Training and Behavior

Back to Basics: Dog Training by Fabian, by Andrea Arden (Howell Book House)

Dog Perfect, by Sarah Hodgson (Howell Book House)

Dr. Dunbar's Good Little Dog Book, by Ian Dunbar (James & Kenneth Publishers)

Surviving Your Dog's Adolescence, by Carol Lea Benjamin (Howell Book House)

The Only Dog Training Book You'll Ever Need, by Gerilyn J. Bielakiewicz (Adams Media)

When Good Dogs Do Bad Things, by Mordecai Siegel (Little, Brown)

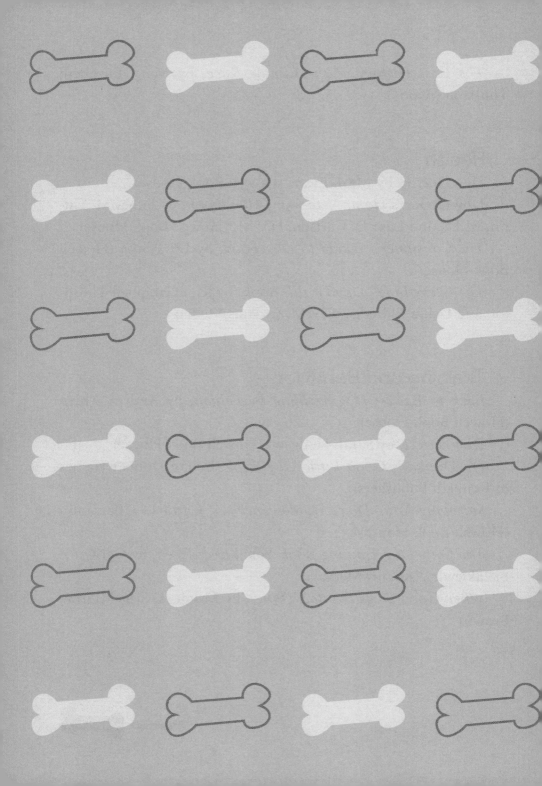

appendix c

Frequently Asked Questions and Vet Answers

You've covered a lot of territory in this organizer, but chances are you still have a lingering question or two. Well, you're not alone! Every dog is different, and even the most experienced dog owners often need advice. This appendix includes a bunch of questions dog owners frequently ask, along with answers from a veterinarian's perspective. It's always better to ask questions than to take chances, so read through this appendix and get the definitive information you need.

Will spaying or neutering change my dog?

Yes, but for the better! Dogs that are spayed or neutered won't contribute to the pet overpopulation problem. The risks of mammary cancer are greatly reduced, and your dog will be free from uterine or testicular cancers. Dogs that are spayed or neutered are more likely to be happy staying at home, less likely to fight, and less likely to mark with their urine.

Why is preventive care stressed?

Preventive care is important for many reasons. Your dog will be healthier if you prevent problems such as parasites and infectious diseases. Your checkbook will also be healthier, as some problems will be totally prevented and any others will be caught early on when treatments tend to be more successful and less expensive.

What concerns should I have before breeding my female dog?

Only dogs that are top-notch, healthy, good examples of their breed should be bred. Your dog should have passed all health screenings for her breed, have been evaluated by knowledgeable judges or breeders, and have a sound temperament. Be prepared to spend a great deal of time and money producing a litter, and realize your dog will be at risk for surgery (C-section) or even death. Have good homes screened and ready ahead of time and be prepared to take any puppies back–even ten years from now!

How often will my dog come into heat?

There is a wide range of normal heat cycles in dogs. Some breeds only cycle once yearly, while others cycle every four months. Check with your breeder for the cycle history of your dog's dam. Many dogs follow their mother's schedule.

I want the biggest, rowdiest puppy. Why is that not a good idea?

While the biggest puppy may grow up just fine, often the big puppies are at higher risk for orthopedic problems. The rowdiest puppy may end up being more dog temperament-wise than the average family wants to deal with. Look for the middle-of-the-road pup as a good family pet.

What should I feed my puppy and how much?

Initially, your puppy should get whatever food the breeder was using. You may want to change over to a different food that you and your veterinarian feel would also be appropriate, but do so gradually. The amounts listed on dog food packaging are just guidelines—you need to adjust the amount to your specific pup and her lifestyle and activity level.

Our family has health insurance. Why can't I get health insurance for my puppy?

Actually, health insurance is available for pets. As with your own insurance, you need to look carefully at the different companies and decide what plan makes sense for you. Some plans cover routine care as well as emergencies, while others are just for serious emergencies and medical illnesses.

How often do I need to bathe my dog?

The number of baths your dog needs varies greatly with his coat type and length and his favorite activities. Shorthaired dogs may need baths to wash off mud and dirt. Longhaired dogs may need baths to help remove dirt and clean the hair. If your dog is groomed on a regular basis, he will need fewer baths. Some dogs with skin problems need frequent baths to keep their skin healthy. Check with your breeder, veterinarian, and groomer about suitable shampoos for your dog.

Why does my dog need to go to the veterinarian every year even if she doesn't need any vaccines?

Just like us, it is important for your dog to have an annual physical (more often for older dogs or dogs with chronic health problems.) At this exam, your veterinarian will check for parasites, discuss your dog's diet and weight with you, and look for any early signs of health problems. Catching problems early means faster and often less expensive treatment.

Which bones in my dog's leg are the same as my wrist? And my ankle?

Your dog's front legs are just like our arms. Come down from the elbow and the next "bendable" area is the carpus, or wrist. Your dog's hind leg is similar to our legs. His hock, or tarsus (the joint that projects backwards above the foot), is the same as your ankle.

What is the difference between a tendon and a ligament?

Ligaments hold bones to bones, while tendons attach muscles to bones. Both are tough, fibrous connective tissues.

Why does my dog cough if she has a heart problem, not a lung problem?

The heart and lungs work very closely together. If your dog has a heart problem that allows fluid to back up in the lungs, she will cough. That cough will not respond to cough medicines but is controlled by diuretics and heart medications.

My dog's urine looks red in the snow. Should I be concerned?

Yes! Normal urine should show up yellow on snow. Red urine is a sign of blood or other pigmented substances like myoglobin (a muscle pigment). Neither of these is normal in urine.

I have a busy work schedule, so I just leave a big bowl of food down all the time for my dog. Is that okay?

Leaving a bowl of food down all the time is not the best way to feed your dog. Food can spoil. Also, your dog may overeat, and you won't be able to tell how much he does eat every day. You could miss signs of illness such as a decreased appetite. It is more difficult to housebreak a puppy when fed like this as well.

My dog loves to beg snacks from me. Can she have extra treats?

Many of our snacks are not the healthiest of foods. Giving your dog salty, fatty, or very sugary treats is not in her best interests. It would be better to keep a small bowl of her treats or food available to give her snacks if you want.

I thought a strong immune system was a good thing, but my veterinarian says my dog has an immune problem. Why is this?

Unfortunately sometimes the immune system gets overstimulated or focused on the wrong tissues-the normal ones instead of outside invaders. When this happens, your dog shows signs of illness from the immune system attacking her own cells.

I thought my dog just had a fatty tumor, but my new veterinarian says it is cancer!

Tumor simply means swelling-it could be a cancer, an abscess, or another kind of swollen tissue. A fatty tumor is a cancer, but luckily, a benign one!

What is a core vaccine and why does my dog need any?

Core vaccines are vaccines that every dog should have. They cover the diseases that are very serious (even life threatening) and that most dogs will get exposed to. These include rabies, distemper, and parvo.

My dog is drinking a lot of water. Is he diabetic?

Certainly diabetes is one disease your veterinarian will test for. Liver and kidney diseases may also make your dog drink more, as well as uterine infections, certain medications, and some endocrine problems.

My dog has a squinted eye. Do I need to worry?

Eye problems can go from minor to serious very quickly. You need to get your dog to the veterinarian. If you can't go right away, at least flush his eye with some artificial tears.

My dog has a genetic problem that is recessive. Would she pass it on to her puppies?

If your dog has a recessive problem, she must have two copies of the defective gene. This means she will pass a defective gene on to all of her pups. Depending on the genetic makeup of her mate, all her pups could show the defect. Or they might appear normal, but all of them will at least carry the defect.

We found fleas on our dog. If we get rid of the dog, will the fleas all leave too?

Getting rid of your dog would be a drastic solution, and it doesn't work. There are flea eggs and larvae in your house now. Unless you treat the environment too, soon you will have flea bites, too. Why not just treat your dog and your house and then start on one of the excellent new flea preventives?

My dog just had abdominal surgery. Can I give her an aspirin for pain?

You need to discuss this with your veterinarian. While aspirin can be excellent for pain, it might increase your dog's chances of oozing around her incision. Your veterinarian can prescribe the safest and most effective pain medications.

My veterinarian has suggested acupuncture for my dog's pain. Don't those needles hurt?

While some dogs do flinch at first from the acupuncture needles, the needles are very small and sharp. Most dogs quickly learn that they feel better from their acupuncture treatments and ignore the needle pricks.

My dog just got hit by a car! What do I do?

First, stay calm. Call your veterinarian's office and tell them you will be on your way. Check quickly for any broken bones that need to be stabilized, any bleeding areas where pressure needs to be applied, and that your dog is breathing. Feel for a pulse or heartbeat, and do CPR if needed. Transport your dog carefully and safely, using a muzzle if needed.

My dog obviously just loves chocolate as she always begs for some of mine. Why shouldn't she have any?

Chocolate can be toxic to dogs—especially dark chocolate and unsweetened baking chocolate. Carob is a safe alternative she can enjoy.

My dog is very old and seems to be in pain. What do I do now?

This is a good time to talk to your veterinarian about hospice care and eventually euthanasia. Discuss ways to make your dog as comfortable as possible, giving him good quality of life for the time he has left.

My dog hates getting her daily medications. Help!

There are many inventive ways to give your dog her pills. Check with your veterinarian to see if her pills can be hidden in treats. Then give one or two normal treats, the doctored treat and another normal one. She ought to be fooled! If that doesn't work, look into getting her long-term medications compounded. There are companies that make medications into treats or even gel to put in her ear.

My male dog is aggressive with other dogs. Would breeding him help?

Absolutely not! Your male dog may become more aggressive after being used for breeding, and no matter what, you don't want to pass that aggressive temperament on.

I work eight hours a day plus have commuting time. Can my four-month-old puppy be left that long?

No, most pups that age can only hold their urine for about four or five hours. Also, that is a long time for a baby to be left with no company. Arrange for a friend, neighbor, or pet sitter to let him out about noon.

My dog has really bad breath. Can I use my mouthwash for her?

Human mouthwash is not good for dogs. They tend to swallow, not gargle, swish, or spit. You need to do some detective work to find out why your dog has bad breath and treat the cause. He may need a dental cleaning or could have a health problem.

My dog sheds all year round. I thought dogs only shed in the spring and fall.

It is true that on a natural schedule, dogs would shed primarily in the spring and fall. But companion dogs live inside and don't get all the natural stimulus for shedding, as they are in a controlled climate. So many of them will shed some hair all year round, shedding slightly greater amounts with seasonal light changes.

My dog has been diagnosed with hypothyroidism. How serious is this?

Hypothyroidism means not enough thyroid hormone is being produced. If this condition is left untreated, it could cause problems for your dog. Luckily, most dogs respond very well to inexpensive thyroid replacement medications.

My dog picks berries off our bushes. Is this okay?

Many dogs seem to love strawberries, blueberries, and raspberries. As long as your dog isn't picking any toxic berries, this is fine. And how clever she is to pick her own!

My dog has bluish purple areas on the pink skin of her belly. Should I worry?

Yes! These areas could easily be hemorrhages under the skin. You should head right to your veterinarian to have her checked for autoimmune problems or bleeding disorders.

My dog has cancer. Can she be treated?

Treatment will depend on the exact type of cancer, but most dogs can handle cancer therapy quite well. Chemotherapy, radiation, and surgery are the most common treatments, alone or in combination.

My puppy just vomited up a long white worm. Do I panic now?

Panic is never a good solution. Save the worm (carefully in a plastic baggie) and take it with a recent stool sample and your pup to the veterinarian. He probably has roundworms and will need a dewormer.

My dog is holding his one ear tipped over. It seems sore, too.

There is a good chance your dog has a hematoma—a blood-filled swelling of his ear. This happens when dogs scratch or shake their ears and break blood vessels. Your dog will need surgery to drain the blood and keep his ear in a normal shape. Your veterinarian will also look for the underlying cause of the shaking or scratching.

A neighborhood dog may have bred my bitch, in addition to the purebred stud I paid for. How do we tell if the pups are purebred?

You can do a DNA profile of the possible sires, dam, and puppy. Comparing profiles will show which puppies had which sire.

My dog got a bee sting and her muzzle is swollen!

First, make sure your dog is breathing normally. Breathing may be a little faster than normal due to excitement, but normal otherwise. If she is, apply a cold compress to her sore muzzle. You may also want to contact your veterinarian about an antihistamine or steroid to reduce the inflammation. If her breathing is labored, hustle to your veterinarian, as she may be having a reaction.

My dog is stiff in the morning. Is this just old age?

Certainly stiffness when getting up can be a symptom of aging. You should have your dog checked for arthritis and look into medications to make him more comfortable.

Why is hydrotherapy good for dogs recovering from lameness?

Hydrotherapy (using a pool or pond) helps keep your dog's muscles fit while keeping weight off the joints.

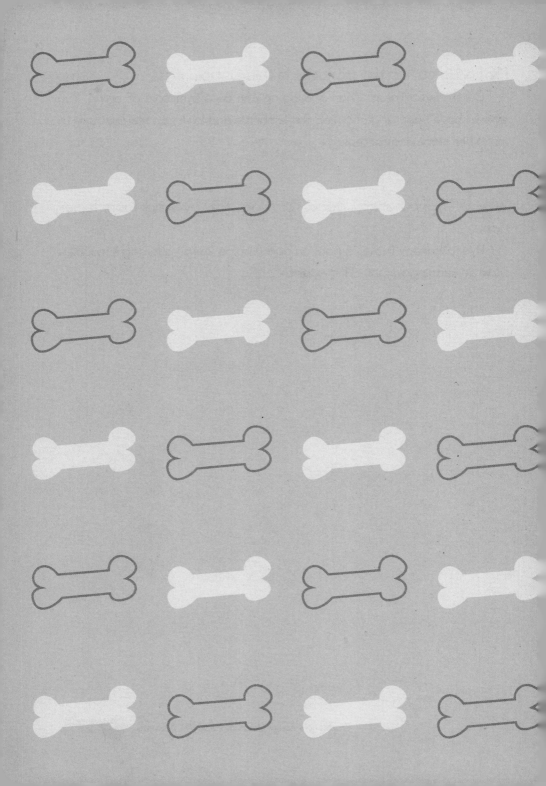